SUCCESSFUL PLAYHOUSES

⌂SUCCESSFUL PLAYHOUSES

John Boeschen

Structures Publishing Company
Farmington, Michigan

Manufactured in the United States of America

Cover photo by Jeff Weissman

Book Design by Carey Ferchland

Current Printing (last digit)
10   9   8   7   6   5   4   3   2   1

ISBN-O-912336-91-9, cloth; 92-7, paper.

**Library of Congress Cataloging
in Publication Data**
Boeschen, John
 Successful playouses.

  Includes index.
  1. Playhouses, Children's — Design and
       construction.
 I. Title
TH4967.B63   690'.8'9   79-16230
 ISBN 0-912336-91-9
 ISBN 0-912336-92-7 pbk.

Contents

Any time of the year, any climate — playhouses provide activity, stimulate a child's imagination and provide a child with his or her own space. (Courtesy Child Life Play Spec.)

Introduction

A magnificent playhouse sits in your backyard. It is three stories high and covered with redwood shingles. Miniature leaded windows gleam in the sunlight and the gabled roof has a natural rock chimney. Your children, however, rarely enter this impressive creation — in fact, they spend most of their time in the backyard playing in a mound of dirt.

What separates the successful from the not-so-successful playhouse? How can you create play spaces that encourage imaginative, enthusiastic play? You will find many suggestions in this book that you can share with your children and that will help you build successful playhouses together.

PLAN AHEAD

Don't build a playhouse scaled for three-year-olds if your children are nine and ten. Three-foot ceilings are fine for tiny tots, but create cramped quarters for a ten-year-old.

The most successful playhouses are often designed by the kids who use them. But an adult hand is sometimes required to transport a 100-pound bag of sand to the backyard, dig a four-foot-deep post hole for a swing, or nail the roof rafters to the wall frame of the treehouse. Even when the job demands your skill and strength, be sure to keep the kids involved. Why not sit down and design that special playhouse with them?

First, sketch a map of your backyard or patio. Make some simple cut-outs of the structures you and the children have in mind (exercise equipment as well as playhouses). Once you've got the right layout (which has a tendency to change as time passes), start building some miniature mock-ups. The models you and the kids build don't have to be fancy. Use cardboard, paperclips, rubber cement, construction paper, tongue depressors, pipe cleaners, toothpicks joined by fresh peas or modeling clay — whatever materials are available and fun to work with. If you and your children agree on a big project (a multi-storied treehouse or a polyhedron city complete with restaurants, gas stations and hotels), draw up blueprints in the fall, build models in the winter, and then do the actual construction in the spring and summer.

Participating in this type of family project stimulates a child's creativity and imagination and, more important, being involved builds self-confidence in kids. When you work with your children, you are telling them, "You're important. I want to hear your ideas and I want you to hear my ideas. Together we're a great team."

LOOKING FOR MATERIALS

Use readily available materials to construct your successful playhouses. Local businesses and tradespeople may even be trying to get rid of the materials you're searching for. A few possibilities include the following:

Carpet stores. Need something warm to put down on the floor of your Tipi or Mongolian yurt? A local carpet outlet may have just the right number of discontinued rug samples. They usually sell for 25¢ or less. You may even be able to obtain larger scrap pieces, thereby saving yourself the trouble of stitching smaller pieces together. Also, foam underpadding remnants are often available.

Construction sites. These are better known as the "poor man's" lumber yard. Nails, studs, siding, sheetrock, 4 x 4's . . . you name it, and you'll probably find it wherever new homes, apartments, or businesses are being built. The materials may not be in perfect condition, but you and your family can put them back into good shape, with little effort.

Gas stations. Lots of "neat kid stuff" — inner tubes, tire casings, bottle caps — can be picked up free at garages. If you live in the country and know a farmer, you can make a fabulous sandbox from an old, discarded tractor tire. Or make a sturdy swing from a truck tire.

Telephone companies. Occasionally you can pick up an old telephone set, the perfect addition to any playhouse. Also, heaps of scrap, colored telephone wire are always plentiful and available. Have your name put on the wooden-cable-spool waiting list. These spools make good tables and are fantastic structures for rolling and climbing. If you're lucky enough to get a large one, you can even turn it into a roundhouse.

Lumber companies. Mounds of wood scraps are given away for the asking. Bizarre-looking curls of wood can dress up the plainest playhouses.

Moving companies. Overseas moving companies occasionally discard large packing crates. These units are generally well built and make excellent playhouse frames. And keep your eyes peeled for those fiberboard drums that movers use to store items in.

Home. If it's been a while since you last cleaned out the garage and closets, your home probably contains a bewildering array of useful items for creative building — old hats, shoes, paper towel rolls, buttons, spools, juice cans, empty plastic detergent bottles, magazines, newspapers, egg cartons, aluminum pie plates — the list is endless.

Have lots of loose objects around. Props encourage kids to explore and experiment: inclines for rolling and pushing; boards and teeters for balancing; pulleys, pumps, and springs for inventing perpetual motion machines. When our son, Deke, was 2½ years old, his favorite plaything was a big, old cardboard box. In the morning hours, he might transform this giant, lightweight carton into a cave surrounded by marauding dinosaurs. In the afternoon, he might add a few sections of garden hose and the cave would become a fire engine. His limitless creations, spurred on and enhanced by a few props, never ceased to amaze my wife and me.

Work with a variety of materials and create surfaces that are warm to the touch, textured, rough, cold, soft or hard. Textures are an important growing experience for a younger child.

DECIDING ON THE STRUCTURE

How permanent do you want the playhouse to be? Will the structure go up on a Saturday and come down on the following Sunday? Or will it be a play space to last for years? If your children are still pre-schoolers and you're thinking of moving within a year, don't build an elaborate miniature townhouse that will become a permanent part of the landscape. A Tipi or a Yurt — something easy to put up, take down and transport to the new home — would be more sensible.

Consider the land. Regardless of how simple or complex the play structure, try to blend it in with the existing natural features of your yard. Take advantage of the slopes, rock outcroppings, and vegetation. Stepping logs or stones on a slope can create varied climbing terrain and hours of motor skill development for your youngsters. Use the existing landforms to help you direct the flow of play and add visual gaiety as well as a feeling of intimacy to play areas.

Climate. How will your structures stand up under changing climate conditions? What steps can you take to assure the playhouse's durability? Will the installation of drainage ditches or the addition of waterproof coverings help? Think in terms, also, of the micro-climate of your particular yard. In order to provide for play that is fun and healthful, you'll have to allow for reasonable amounts of sun, shade and protection from the wind.

Defining territory. Decide what part of your yard belongs to you and what part belongs to the kids. A sense of territoriality is important to children. And the playhouse should be a place they can go to get away from the pressures of homework and parental demands.

If possible, try to position the play units of older kids (eight years and up) out of sight of the main house. Kids at this age are beginning to vigorously assert their own personalities, and they need opportunities to be physically apart from their parents. The spatial needs of the under-five child, however, are much more limited. Their play area should be within sight and shouting distance of the house . . . and in an area protected from motor traffic. If your children are physically or emotionally handicapped, you may want to locate their playspace closer to the main house regardless of age. Skillful placement and design of playhouses and exercise apparatus can make children unaware of their parents' proximity, fostering feelings of independence. Children with mental retardation and brain injuries, as well as kids with neuromuscular and orthopedic handicaps, generally need more closely-contained areas for monitoring.

Keep imagination in mind. Leave part of the design open so that your children can add onto it and grow with the structure. You can build the basic frame (sink the corner posts of an A-frame into the ground) and let the kids put up the siding, paint and decorate. Allow their creative imaginations free reign.

TOOLS

A craftsperson is known by the tools he keeps. To build children's play areas, you'll need tools for measuring, cutting, fastening and striking. Measure and mark before you begin any project. A good rule to follow is: "measure twice, cut once". Measuring tools that will help you do the job right include a combination square, pocket tape rule, long tape, level and carpenter's square.

Once you've measured, the next step usually requires cutting. Only the right tool will produce the results you're after. Hand saws are best for crosscutting and ripping. Back saws and mitre box saws produce accurate joints with their finer teeth. Compass and keyhole saws have narrow, tapered blades for making curves or inside cuts starting from a bored hole. For boring holes perpendicular to the surface you're working on, a brace and bit is indispensable. You also can use a hand drill for drilling wood, metal and plastic. Jack planes, another cutting tool, are used for edge straightening, smoothing rough surfaces and beveling edges. Surform tools are used like jack planes, but are less expensive. They also can be used file-fashion on aluminum, brass, copper, plastic, wood and other materials.

Screwdrivers are probably the most popular and easy-to-use fastening tools. All screwdrivers should be matched to screw size. For example,

A well equipped workshop should include tools from each of the basic tool categories: measuring, cutting, fastening and striking. (Courtesy The Stanley Works, Inc.)

you'll need at least two Phillips screwdrivers to handle an average range of Phillips screw sizes. Working in cramped quarters requires an offset screwdriver.

The best tool you can find for nailing and nail-pulling is the curved claw hammer. Thirteen to twenty ounce hammers, designed for general carpentry, are your best bets. You should have a nail set to drive the potentially hazardous heads of finishing nails out-of-sight and below the wood's surface. Nail sets come in two basic varieties: round and square (the square-headed variety doesn't bounce off the nail when you're working at an angle).

The tools just described should be part of your basic tool kit. If you're a serious do-it-yourselfer, you also might consider purchasing the following for projects in this book: wood-cutting chisels, side-cutting pliers, C-clamps, vise, propane torch, electric drill, portable power saw, jigsaw and finishing sander. *(See Successful Tools for Home-owners by James Ritchie).*

1
Treehouses

Children live in a world of giants . . . parents, furniture, cars, houses. Kids are constantly being looked down at while they, in turn, are constantly straining to see the tops of things. Treehouses turn this belittling situation on its head. Perched high up in the canopy of a great tree, children take on the role of giants . . . they look down at a small world that squints up into the bright sky to catch glimpses of them. Treehouses give children new perspectives on their environment.

Treehouses offer even more: they give the "gang" a place to get away from it all . . . a secret place among the green foliage. This privacy also encourages creative daydreaming and provides a cozy spot for reading. Perhaps most important, treehouses are just plain fun. Once the last plank is nailed in place, the treehouse can become a crow's nest on a pirate ship, the control module of a starship or the castle of a mighty jungle lord.

SELECTING A TREE

What makes a good site for a treehouse? According to the experts, the best supporting points are provided by trees whose main trunk divides into two or more major limbs about eight feet from the base. The most stable treehouses are built into a tree where at least three points (preferably four points) of the tree are on the same level. These points support the corners of the treehouse's platform. Deciduous trees — Those that shed their leaves at least once a year — are your best bets and remember that the trees must be sturdy, sound and suitable for the treehouse. Most pines will not meet this criteria; they are too messy and seldom have a minimum of three points at the same level.

A tree with a minimum of three points at the same level makes the best site for your treehouse.

Once you've found the perfect tree, treat it with care. Put in as few holes as possible because holes can be dangerous to the life of the tree. There's a difference of opinion among experts whether to use nails or screws. Some advocate the use of nails because they are less rigid than screws, giving the tree some room for motion. Others claim that nails are more likely to pull out completely; consequently, three nails are required

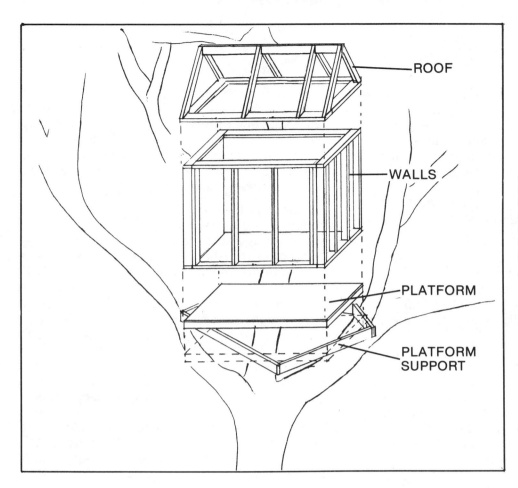

ROOF

WALLS

PLATFORM

PLATFORM
SUPPORT

Figure 1

Supporting beams must be level if the crow's nest or treehouse platform is to sit straight. Use a carpenter's level to check before screwing the beams into place.

to replace just one screw. I feel that the use of screws, with considerable consideration being given to the use of lag screws, is generally preferable to nails, but situations vary from tree to tree.

SAFETY CONSIDERATIONS

Whatever materials you work with, avoid the temptation to cut into the tree. If you accidently notch or tear off some bark from the trunk or one of the limbs, you can speed healing with a simple technique. With sharp knife in hand, cut away any loose bark around the wound in the shape of a diamond. Paint over this wound with tree paint (tree paint is formulated to stop decay and keep out pesky insects and disease-producing organisms).

Take care of yourself, too! Don't leave tools in a tree where they might fall out and injure someone below. Avoid standing on dead branches — it is best to remove them before starting any major construction. Keep out of trees that stand close to electrical and telephone wires. When you work high up in a tree, wear a safety belt to prevent falls. Always be on the look-out for the glossy, green leaves of poison ivy (the leaves turn a reddish hue in Autumn). And keep clear of all trees and treehouses during a rain or thunder storm.

Other rules to remember: 1) lift materials correctly with knees bent; 2) avoid wearing loose clothing; 3) don't use power tools on wet ground; 4) wear goggles and safety glasses when necessary; and, 5) be sure all your tools are in top working condition.

One last rule and perhaps the most important of all. Children under seven years of age should not play in treehouses tucked high up in a tree. Youngsters of this age do not possess the physical coordination necessary to safely manuever in swaying places high off the ground. But there are safe alternatives for the under-seven crowd. You'll find treehouse plans for this age group further along in the chapter.

SIMPLE TREEHOUSES

The most basic treehouse you can build is the crow's nest. Named after the shelter for the lookout man perched high atop the mast of an ocean-going vessel, the crow's nest will make a great secret clubhouse or hideout.

The first part of the crow's nest to build is the supporting platform which will serve as the foundation for the floor. But before you spring into the tree of your choice and start piecing together the framework, take some advice from one who has fallen from high, leafy places and build your platform on the ground! When it's finished, you and your helpers can hoist it into position.

You'll need the following tools to build your crow's nest. Hammer; hand saw; tape measure; screw driver; bit & brace; and level.

Materials required. 2x4's, 2x3's, wood screws and/or lag screws, common nails and flooring planks (1x6 — 1x12) or ½" exterior plywood. (Tree sites and kids vary in size; therefore, no exact dimensions are given. Build according to the size of your kids and the tree.)

INSTRUCTIONS

1. Determine the distances between the three or four points of your tree's main supporting branches. Saw three or four (depending on the number of points your tree has) 2x4's to fit the span between supporting points.

2. Screw one end of a 2x4 beam (sill) into the tree. Now, with the aid of a level, screw the other end of the same beam in place. Repeat this procedure with the remaining support beams. Be certain that all your beams are level, or your completed crow's nest will not sit squarely.

3. Once back on the ground, build the platform that will rest atop the supporting beams. Use four 2x3's to make the frame. Construct the frame so that it rests securely on the 2x4 supporting beams.

4. Reinforce the corners of the platform with framing clips or truss clips.

5. When you've assembled the platform frame, make the flooring from 1x6's — 1x12's or from ½" exterior grade plywood cut to size.
   The platform can be pretty heavy, so be sure you get help hoisting it up to the supporting beams. Or if you prefer, the frame can be hoisted into the tree and the flooring added later. Once the platform is up in the tree, move it around until it rests firmly on the 2x4 supporting beams (see Fig. 1). Nail the platform to the beams with 4-inch long common nails.

6. With the platform in place, add four walls cut from ½-inch exterior grade plywood. Screw these walls to the outside edge of the platform and secure the upper corner joints with clips. Be sure to leave an opening of at least 12 inches in one of the sides for an entrance way. The walls should be at least 37 inches high for an eight-year-old. As a general rule of thumb, wall height should be increased ten percent for each additional year of user age.

Entrance to the crow's nest can be achieved by wooden, metal or rope ladder (avoid screwing or nailing wooden steps into the trunk of the tree—this practice may harm the tree). For example, a simple rope ladder can be made by cutting 1"x4" wooden rungs 12 inches long. Drill a hole at each end of the rungs just wide enough for the rope to pass through. Tie one knot at the same spot on each length of rope, then slip the wooden rung into place. Tie off another knot 12 inches up from the first step on both rope lengths and slide the next step into place. Continue this process until your ladder is complete. Fasten the upper ends of the ladder securely to the crow's nest using heavy-duty eye-bolts. Because rope ladders are hard to master unless they're anchored at the base, it is a good idea to stake the dangling ends into the ground.

WOOD-FRAME TREEHOUSE

If the kids want more space and protection from sun, wind and rain, you can help them build a real tree palace. For the past hundred years or so, most of the homes in the United States have been constructed with frames made from many thin segments of lumber which make good, sturdy skeletons for treehouses. In addition to the materials required to build a simple treehouse, you will need 2"x3" strips for your "tree palace."

INSTRUCTIONS

1. Cut two equal lengths of 2"x3" strips to run the length of one of the platform's edges. These two runners, top place and bottom sill plate, will hold wall studs in place. Leaving a space of ½" between both ends of the strips and the platform edge. This space will help support any siding that goes onto the treehouse frame.

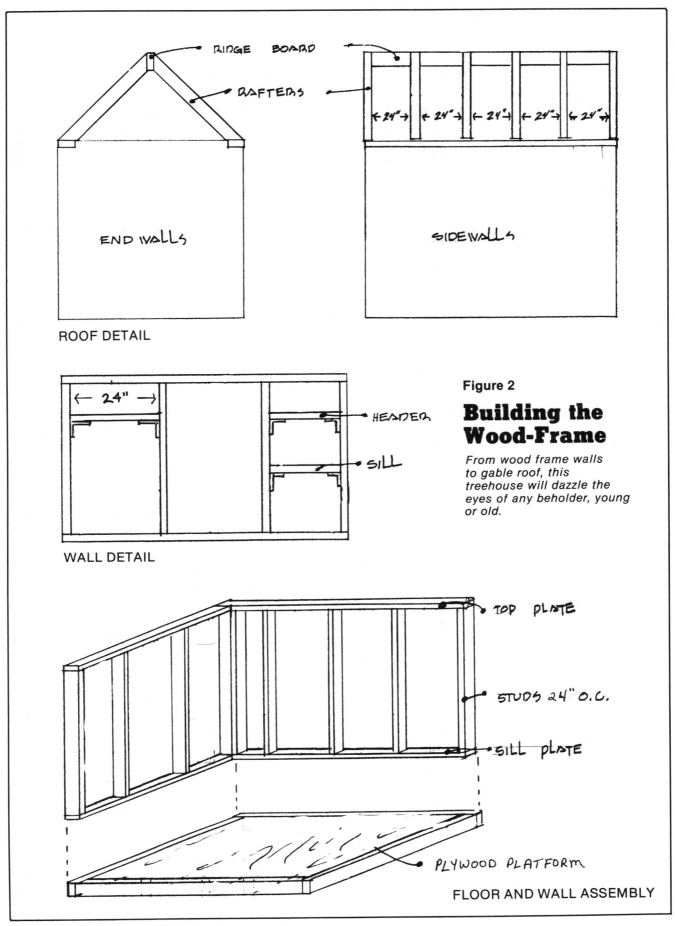

RIDGE BOARD

RAFTERS

END WALLS

SIDEWALLS

← 24" → ← 24" → ← 24" → ← 24" → ← 24" →

ROOF DETAIL

← 24" →

HEADER

SILL

WALL DETAIL

Figure 2

Building the Wood-Frame

From wood frame walls to gable roof, this treehouse will dazzle the eyes of any beholder, young or old.

TOP PLATE

STUDS 24" O.C.

SILL PLATE

PLYWOOD PLATFORM

FLOOR AND WALL ASSEMBLY

2. Use your hand saw to cut the wall studs from additional lengths of 2"x3" strips. The studs should be high enough to satisfy your children's safety needs (37" for an eight-year-old; ten percent higher for each additional year of age).

3. Make pencil marks twenty-four inches apart on both the top and bottom runners. Assemble the wall by nailing studs at each end of the runners and then on center at each of the 24" marks.

4. Repeat steps 1-3 for the facing wall.

5. Repeat steps 1-4 for the two remaining sides (be sure to leave a ½" space all along the outer edge of the platform as a supporting surface for siding).

6. Now you're ready to put the wall frames into place. Drive 2" common nails through the bottom wall runner into the platform (the platform already is nailed into place on the supporting beams — it's the same as the one you built for the crow's nest). The first few nails should only be driven in halfway — this will allow you to easily straighten any walls that are out of line. Once you're positive the walls are properly aligned, drive the nails all the way into the platform frame. Secure the upper corners of the touching wall frames with 2" common nails.

7. No tree palace is complete without an entrance. Adding a door is an easy matter. Simply add a header at kid height between any two of the studs (see Fig. 2). If you cover the frame with ½" exterior playwood, be sure to cut out the door opening before nailing the siding into place. (Add a safety rope across the doorway entrance. Secure the rope halfway up one side of the door with an eyebolt. The free end of the rope, complete with a safety spring latch, can be fastened securely to a second eyebolt screwed into the opposite side of the door frame).

8. Add windows using the same procedure. Nail a header and a sill between any two studs to create the window opening (see Fig. 2). Again if you cover your treehouse fame with ½" exterior plywood, be sure to first cut out the window opening in the siding.

You've gone this far, why not go all the way and add a gable roof! A gable roof sheds water in the winter months and allows the owners to stretch to their full heights. It is a roof that will dazzle the beholder.

INSTRUCTIONS FOR THE GABLE ROOF

1. The first thing you'll want to cut are the roof rafters. Measure each rafter 0.71 times the width of your treehouse (if the treehouse is six feet wide, each rafter will be 6' x 0.71 = 4.26'). Carefully cut both ends of each rafter at an angle of 45 degrees.

2. Cut another length of 2"x3" firring strip to make the ridge board (the beam that forms the peak of the roof). While still on the ground, nail two rafters at either end of the ridge board (see Fig. 2).

3. Using all the help you can muster, raise high the ridge board and four rafters. Once in place, nail the loose end of each rafter to the wall frame of the treehouse.

4. Add additional rafters every 24 inches until the gable roof is complete.

5. Cover with ½" exterior grade plywood, 1"x6" — 1"x12" siding or tempered masonite and the treehouse is ready for occupancy.

SIMPLE SWING

No tree with a treehouse would be complete without a swing. Besides providing hours of pleasure and physical activity, a swing helps younger children develop muscular coordination and a sense of rhythm.

You can make the seat for the swing from a discarded car or truck tire. Simply loop the supporting rope around the tire and tie it tightly. But you'll have to inspect the swing regularly because the bead of the tire eventually will eat through the rope. A better method of attaching the rope to the tire is to fit a 12" length of 2x4 to the inside of the tire. Then, using a $^{15}/_{16}$" auger whose square bottom has been cut off so that it fits a power drill, bore a hole through the 2x4's center and the tire bead. Slip the rope through both and secure with a strong knot.

Suspend the tire with ¾" hemp rope or ½" nylon or polyethylene cord (these will give you a minimum of 1000 pounds load support) from a sturdy tree branch. Be sure to cover the supporting branch with a piece of scrap tread to protect the bark from the wear and tear of the moving rope.

If kids in wheelchairs are to have easy access to the swing, lengthen the supporting ropes or cables. Children with neuromuscular and ortho-

Built with safety foremost in mind, these swings are designed for younger children. Note the high backs and sturdy arm supports. The swing on the right has its protective, wooden seat belt in place.

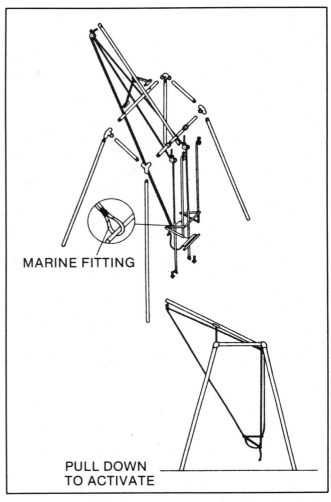

MARINE FITTING

PULL DOWN
TO ACTIVATE

*This swing gives kids unable to pump control over their swinging motion. Joe Bonner, designer. (Courtesy **A Playground for All Children**, New York Dept. of City Planning)*

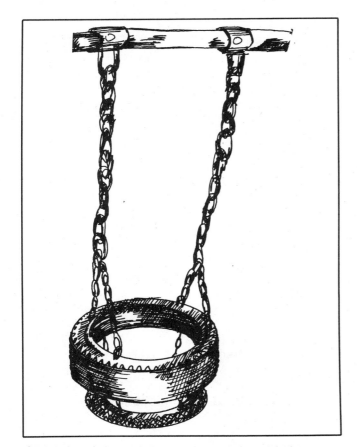

A two-tiered tire swing provides much needed support for pre-schoolers or handicapped children.

pedic handicaps also may need special back and arm supports because of poor sitting balance. One solution is a two-tiered tire swing. This swing can be made from a small diameter tire (from a compact car) suspended from a larger truck tire. The lower tire acts as the seat and the upper as the back and arm support.

Test the swing yourself to make certain everything is positioned properly, but always let your children have the last say as to whether the arrangement is satisfactory. If they are uncomfortable and apprehensive, let them help you modify the swing to their own special needs.

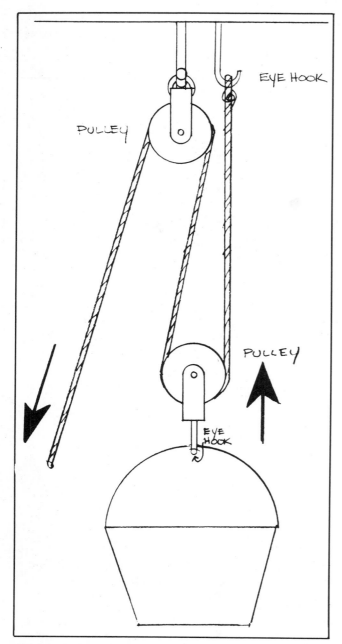

PULLEY

EYE HOOK

PULLEY

EYE HOOK

A combination fixed and movable pulley makes lifting heavy treasures into the treehouse a snap. The top pulley is called a fixed pulley and the bottom one is called a movable pulley.

HAMMOCKS AND PULLEYS

With the treehouse and the swing completed you're going to need a rest. Try stretching a hammock between two trees or rigid up-rights. Then lay back and relax . . . if you can keep the kids out of the hammock! Hammocks are a challenge to growing youngsters. The swaying motion of a hammock is similar to the rocking motion of a small boat on rough seas and takes a great deal of body coordination to stay aboard. Children in hammocks can pretend they are stranded at sea on a life raft or on a space voyage temporarily endangered by an ion storm.

While you rest in your hammock, the kids will need some additional help hauling furniture and other valuables into the treehouse. You can help them lighten the load by constructing a combination fixed and movable pulley. You'll need two ordinary clothesline pulleys, two eye-hooks and a length of rope. Set up the system as illustrated.

With this handy little lift, chairs and even tables can be easily raised to the treehouse. If you want to carry more with each load, attach an empty wooden crate, basket or cardboard box to the rope and you've got yourself a modified version of the traditional "dumb-waiter." The dumb-waiter makes a great prop for imaginary play. It can be used to pull victims of a capsized boat to safety, lower supplies to a jungle research team, or to descend to the molten core of the earth.

One last suggestion for your palace in the tree or your humble crow's nest is a telephone. You could hook up a real one with two old discards from the phone company and a six-volt dry cell, but there's an easier way to do it. Take a long section of garden hose or surgical tubing — enough to stretch from the ground to the treehouse — and attach two plastic funnels, one at each end. Talk softly into one funnel and your voice will travel through the tubing and be heard quite distinctly at the other receiver.

TREELESS TREEHOUSES

Not all treehouses need to roost in the arms of a friendly tree.

Designer Paul W. Mastenbroek of Woodbridge, Ontario, has built a treeless treehouse out of 5/8" redwood plywood that gives kids a unique bird's-eye view of their world. The view is accomplished through the use of four 30" diameter, clear acrylic domes.

Mastenbroek, who built the unusual treehouse for his three preschoolers, used a 6x6 hemlock pole to support the playhouse. He set the pole in five feet of subsurface concrete for greater stability. The house stands just about six feet above the ground (the overall height is eleven feet). Kids clammer up a ladder secured to the pole and through an opening in the floor for quick and easy access.

The "Treeless" Treehouse

Children get a birds-eye view of the world from this sturdy treeless treehouse. Designer Paul Mastenbroek used 3/8'' redwood plywood, 6x6 hemlock, some lumber scraps and four acrylic domes. Plans are shown below and on page 18 for Mastenbroek's treehouse. The entire project cost less than $100 to build. (Courtesy Simpson Timber)

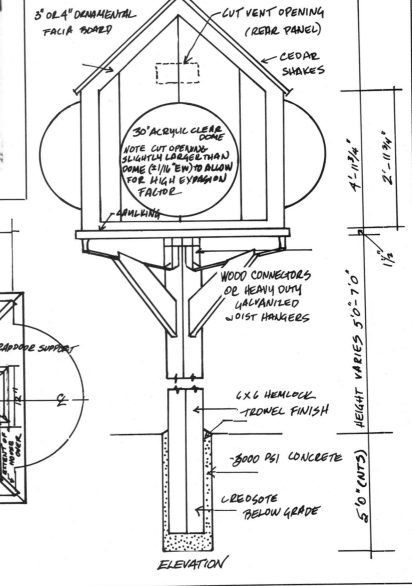

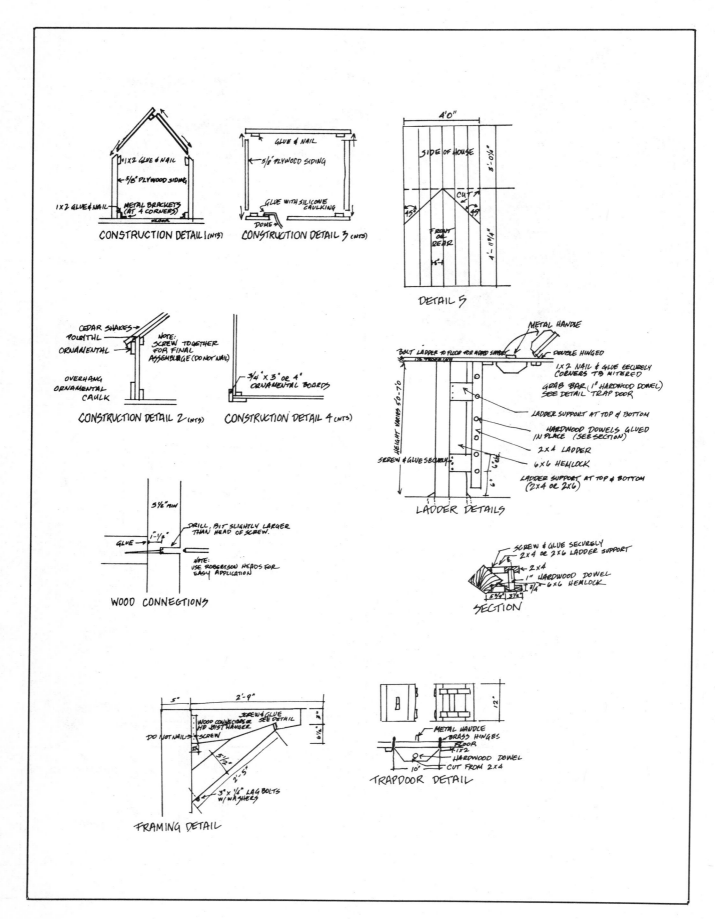

CONSTRUCTION DETAIL 1 (NTS)

CONSTRUCTION DETAIL 3 (NTS)

DETAIL 5

CONSTRUCTION DETAIL 2 (NTS)

CONSTRUCTION DETAIL 4 (NTS)

WOOD CONNECTIONS

LADDER DETAILS

SECTION

FRAMING DETAIL

TRAPDOOR DETAIL

The Tower Fort

This Tower Fort stimulates dramatic play and encourages social interaction. (Courtesy American Plywood Association)

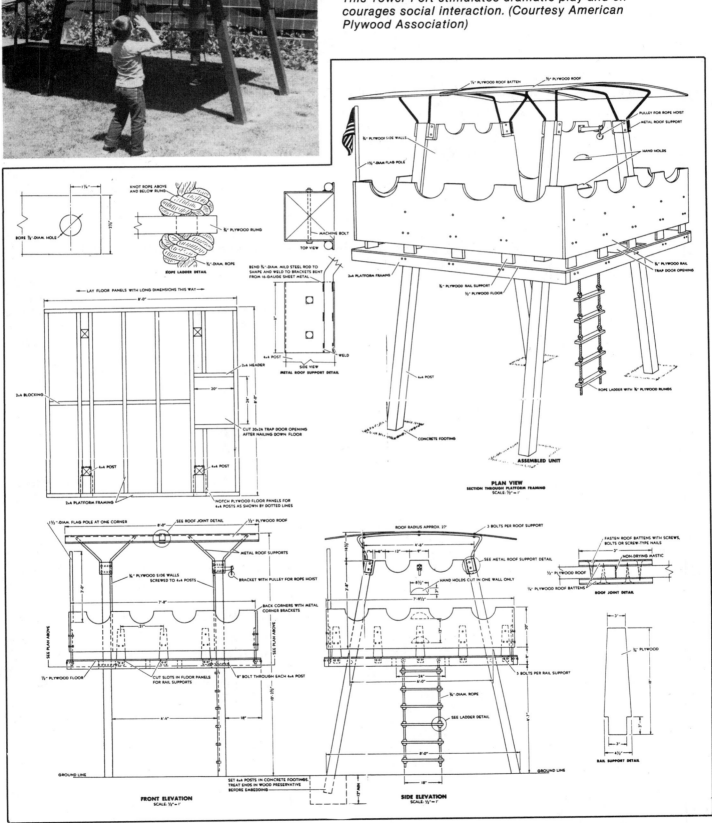

TOWER FORT

The backyard tower fort, a treeless treehouse resting on four uprights, is another easy-to-build structure that'll capture your kids' imaginations the moment they haul up the rope ladder. Suddenly they're holding down Fort Apache, guiding a space freighter between planets, or sailing a pirate ship in search of buried treasure.

Building the backyard tower fort is an easy job when you take the work a step at a time. The draw-ing of the assembled tower shows how the structure fits together. Plan and elevation drawings supply all needed dimensions. Cutting diagrams indicate how to lay out the parts on standard 4'x 8' panels of exterior-type plywood.

Look at the side elevation drawing. You'll see that the platform of the tower is built around four 4''x 4'' posts. Each pair of posts is spaced at the top with a ¾'' plywood side-wall to make an A-shaped frame. Setting up these A-frames is the first step in construction. The platform is then framed-in around them.

Two panels of ½'' plywood are used to deck the platform framing. Rail supports bolted to the in-side faces of 2x4's hold up ¾'' plywood rails. A rope ladder hung from the platform framing leads up to a trap door opening in the plywood floor.

The curved, 8'-square roof (two panels of ½'' plywood joined with battens) mounts on special metal brackets bolted to the tops of the 4x4 posts. Be sure to get completely waterproof exterior ply-wood. Buy galvanized fastenings.

It's easiest to pre-cut the plywood before begin-ning actual construction. Lay out the panels using a straight-edge and large carpenter's square. Re-member to allow two saw kerfs (the width of two saw blades) when measuring dimensions. While you can cut out the parts with a hand saw, using a portable electric circular saw saves considerable time.

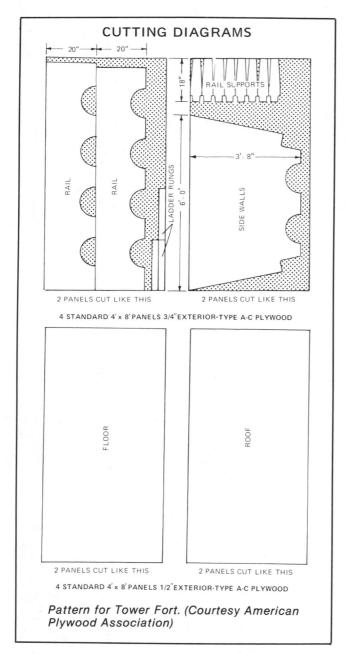

Pattern for Tower Fort. (Courtesy American Plywood Association)

MATERIALS

Plywood
2 panels, ¾''x4'x8'—Ext-ADA • A-C, (side walls, rails)
2 panels, ½''x4'x8'—Ext-ADA • A-C, (roof, floor)
2 strips, ¼''x3''x8'—Ext-ADA • A-C, (roof battens)

Lumber
40 linear feet, 4''x4'' four 10' lengths, (posts)
88 linear feet, 2''x4'' eleven 8' lengths, (platform framing)
1 piece, 1½''D. one 3' length dowel, (flagpole)

Hardware and Miscellaneous
1 approximately 9'' long bracket with pulley, rope hoist)
2 assembled per plan — metal roof supports, (support roof)
4 — ¾''x3''x3'' — metal corner braces, (rail corners)
4 — ½''D.x8'' — carriage bolts, (framing bolts)
32 — ¼''D.x3'' — carriage bolts, (rail support fastenings)

60—¼"D.x2" — carriage bolts, (rail & roof
fastenings)
8—⅜"D.x4½" — machine bolts, (roof support
fastenings)
2—⅜"D.x2" — eye bolts, (rope ladder)
12'—¾"D. — manila rope, (rope ladder)
6d galvanized box or casing nails
Screws, bolts or screw-type nails as required

INSTRUCTIONS
FOR BUILDING THE TOWER FORT

1. Building identical A-frames to support the
tower platform is the first step. To assemble
them, arrange four 4x4's in pairs flat on the
ground, spacing each pair as shown in the side
elevation. Measure down from the tops to es-
tablish a ground line, and at this line tack a strip
of scrap lumber across each pair of 4x4's. Next
fasten a ¾" plywood side-wall across the top
of the 4x4's with No. 8, 1½" F.H. wood screws.
Then bolt 2"x4" crosspieces — part of the platform framing — across each frame on a line exactly 4'7" above ground level.

2. When you've selected a suitable location for
your tower, measure off an 8' square and at
each corner dig holes at least a foot deep for
concrete footings. Set scrap lumber forms in
the holes. Old boxes will serve.

   Treat the ends of the 4x4's that will be embedded in concrete with creosote or another
wood preservative. Then lift the A-frames into
position, resting them on the scrap-lumber
strips nailed across them at ground level, to
suspend the lower ends of the 4x4's in the
forms. Rig temporary diagonal bracing set
against stakes to hold the frames erect. Then,
when you're satisfied that they're accurately
aligned and plumbed, pour concrete mix into
the forms around the bases of the 4x4's.

3. When the concrete has hardened, frame in the
platform with 2x4's, cutting in headers and fitting blocking as shown in the plan drawing.

   Next, lay the two ½" plywood floor panels,
which butt on the blocking. It's necessary to
notch the floor panels, as indicated by the dotted lines on the plan, in order to fit them around
the 4x4 posts. Save the pieces cut from the
notches. After nailing down the floor, trim these
pieces to fit against the 4x4's and replace

them. Next saw out the trap door opening flush
with the headers and framing.

   The ¾" plywood rail supports are mounted in
slots cut in the floor and bolted to the framing.
Cut these slots with an auger, keyhole saw and
square rasp. After bolting the supports, mark
and drill bolt holes in the ¾" plywood rails. Reinforce the rail at the corners with metal corner
braces.

4. If you own metalworking equipment, you can
make the special metal fixtures yourself to support the roof. If you don't, have a welding shop
make them for you. While dimensions aren't
critical, the arched rods should align reason-
ably well.

   Bent roughly to the shape shown in the eleva-
tions, these rods are welded to heavy sheet-
metal brackets. Drill three holes for roof bolts
in each rod. After priming the supports with
top-grade metal primer, give them two coats of
asphalt-base paint. Then bolt them to the top
ends of the 4x4 posts.

   Join the ½" plywood roof panels with battens as shown in the roof joint detail. It's easiest to paint the roof before mounting it. When
it's painted, lift the roof into place, bend it
across the supports, and bolt it down. Dab the
bolts with asphalt paint.

   Fasten a 3' length of heavy dowel in one
corner of the rail for a flagpole, and saw out
hand-holes in the side-wall above the trap door
opening. On the same wall, mount a pulley on a
suitable bracket, which the youngsters will use
to haul up supplies. Finally, hang a rope ladder
from heavy eye-bolts fastened to the platform
framing in the trap door opening.

5. Finish your tower fort inside and out with top-
quality exterior house paint. A three-coat finish
(house paint undercoat followed with two finish
coats) weathers best.

MOVEMENT EXPLORER

Most playhouses, whether they are treehouses
or tower forts, function best when used primarily
for social play. The Movement Explorer, designed
by the Stanley Works for kids 3-12, is a unique
jungle gym that supplements backyard social
play with opportunities for the rough and tumble
activities of growing children. For example, the
unit's adjustable cross beams are great for climb-

Treeless treehouses can take many different forms. They can be constructed from heavy timber in post-and-beam fashion, from reused telephone poles and logs, or from giant cable spools.

ing and double as sturdy balance beams. Because of their varying lengths and heights, the beams serve all age and skill levels.

The movement explorer is more than just an exercise apparatus. It's a learning device that, among other things, can help your children acquire the skills necessary for reading and writing.

Your children become aware of their bodies through movement activities. They discover how the right and left sides work together in a coordinated way. This ability to distinguish left and right is known as laterality and is usually acquired at five or six years of age. A child needs laterality to perform more sophisticated tasks that require a left to right sequential flow, such as reading and writing.

Stanley recommends that you use No. 2 Douglas fir for all major components in the movement explorer. Coat all lumber with a wood preservative (such as Cuprinol) before assembling and after cutting to size and boring holes. Or you can make your own mixture from penetrating oil, penetrating water seal primer, thinner, and boiled linseed oil. Mix together in a ratio of 1:1:1:2.

Smooth sharp corners, edges and rough spots on all lumber with a surform tool and sandpaper. Use only galvanized fasteners and hardware to prevent rusting. All nails, screws and nuts should be countersunk. Before your kids use the move-

ment explorer, make sure all fastenings are tight and that there are no exposed nuts, sharp corners, rough spots, or anything else that could cause injury.

The Movement Explorer

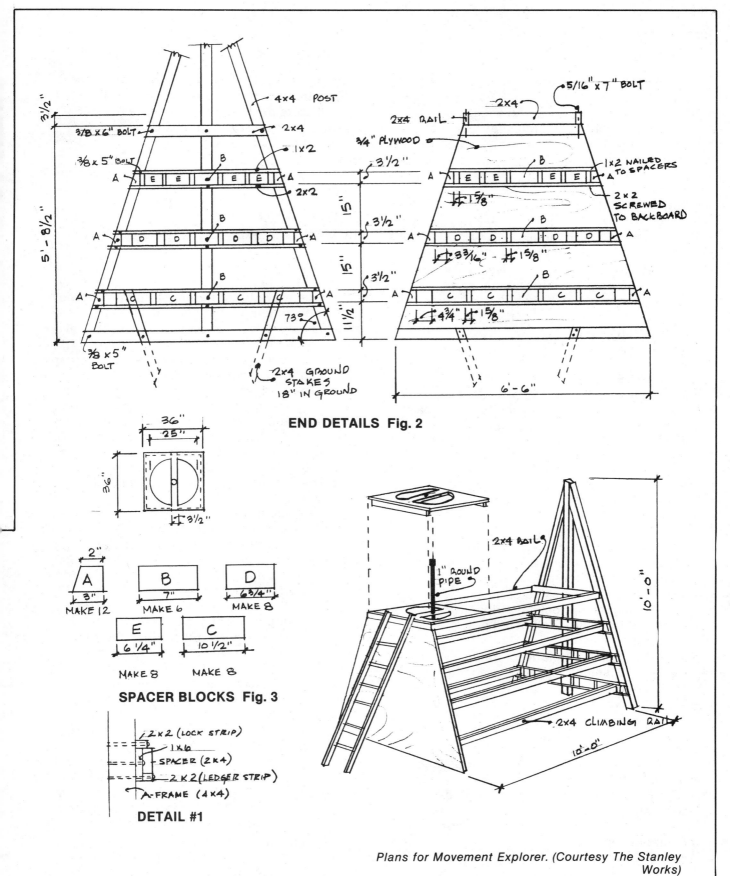

END DETAILS Fig. 2

SPACER BLOCKS Fig. 3

A — 2" / 3" — MAKE 12
B — 7" — MAKE 6
D — 6 3/4" — MAKE 8
E — 6 1/4" — MAKE 8
C — 10 1/2" — MAKE 8

DETAIL #1

2 x 2 (LOCK STRIP)
1 x 6
SPACER (2 x 4)
2 x 2 (LEDGER STRIP)
A-FRAME (4 x 4)

Plans for Movement Explorer. (Courtesy The Stanley Works)

Most major elements are assembled with carriage bolts, washers and nuts. Plans show length and location of these bolts. Adjust the depth of counterbore according to thickness of material and bolt length. You must make counterbores before you drill bolt holes.

TOOLS

claw hammer	brace with ¼", ⁵⁄₁₆", ½"
tape rule	and 1¼" bits
steel square	screwdrivers
combination square	surform or plane
level	¾" or 1" wood chisel
cross cut saw	nail set
keyhole/compass saw	

MATERIALS

2 — 4'x8'x ¾" exterior fir plywood for backboard
1 — 4'x8'x ¾" exterior fir plywood for climbing pole platform
1 — 1"x6"x12' for crosspiece backstop
2 — 1"x6"x10' for crosspiece backstop
3 — 2"x4"x10' No. 2 fir for spacer blocks
1 — 2"x4"x10' No. 2 fir for top and bottom of backboard
1 — 2"x2"x12' No. 2 fir for ledger strips
2 — 2"x2"x10' No. 2 fir for ledger strips
1 — 2"x2"x6' No. 2 fir for locking strips
1 — 2"x2"x10' No. 2 for locking strips
1 — 1"x2"x6' pine for locking strips
1 — 1"x2"x10' pine for locking strips
1 — 2"x4"x8' No. 2 fir for climbing pole platform frame
1 — 1"x4"x36" pine for platform frame
14 — 2"x4"x10' select structural grade fir for climbing rails
1 — 2"x4"x8' No. 2 fir for tie-downs

Hardware

9 — ⅜"x6" carriage bolts for ledger strips (add washers under nuts)
21 — ⅜"x6" carriage bolts for spacer blocks (add washers under nuts)
9 — ⅜"x5" carriage bolts for locking strips (add washers under nuts)
4 — ⁵⁄₁₆"x7" carriage bolts for top rails (add washers under nuts)
1 box No. 10 1¼" galvanized flat head screws
4 — No. 10 3½" flat head screws

10' length galvanized iron pipe one inch inside diameter threaded at one end with cap. Check pipe before purchase to make sure it is 100% smooth and free from rough spots.
1 lb. — 8d galvanized common nails

INSTRUCTIONS FOR BUILDING MOVEMENT EXPLORER

Study the diagrams. The two top rails and two bottom outside rails of this unit are fixed. All other rails can be moved to different locations in order to change climbing arrangement. The movable feature is achieved by setting the end of the rails in slots formed with 2"x4" spacer blocks. The rails are supported at each end by a 2"x2" ledger strip which also serves as a base for the spacer blocks. The ledger strip and blocks on the plywood backboard are fastened to the plywood with screws run in from the outside face of the plywood. At the A-frame end the ledger strips are bolted to the frame over a 1"x6" backstop that replaces the 2"x4" crosspiece (see detail at top of Fig. 2). The spacer blocks are held by screws run through the 1"x6".

Rails are held down at each end with a locking strip so they can't jump out of the slots. Locking strips at the plywood end are nailed in place. The 2"x2" locking strips at the A-frame end are held in place with bolts and nuts that can be removed to change the arrangement of rails.

According to the Western Wood Products Association, a single length of select structural Douglas fir, 10 feet long, in the dimensions given here and set on edge, will support 43 pounds per linear foot or 214 pounds as a concentrated load at the center. If more than this amount of weight will be imposed on the rails, double all single rails.

Make up the plywood backboard and install the crosspieces at top and bottom. Install ledger strips. Install 1"x6" backstop and ledger strips on A-frame. Set the plywood backboard in place and install two top and two bottom outside rails. Top rails are bolted to 2"x4" crosspiece at each end. Run screws through 1"x6" into end of bottom rails. Install tie-downs.

Cut the adjustable climbing rails so there will be about ¾" play at one end to make it easy to lift them out of the slots.

Make the spacer blocks (see Fig. 3). You'll have to adjust the length of each block slightly to compensate for variance in the thickness of lumber. Leave enough space between blocks so that rails can lift out even when the wood has expanded from moisture. Install fixed and movable locking strips.

Construct the frame for top platform and climbing pole. Use a keyhole, compass or sabre saw to cut out climbing openings and pole hole in plywood platform. Insert climbing pole and drive into ground.

Even though this wooden structure is built for rough use, normal wear and tear will take its toll. A few simple precautions will add years to the life of all your wooden creations. When you set units up outside, keep an eye on the weather and be prepared with a plastic cover. Long term maintenance is a matter of sanding and varnishing once a year. Smooth down the worn spots and make sure all sanded areas are clean and dry before you spread on varnish. For an exceptionally protective finish, apply a clear or pigmented polyurethane.

For additional free information on Stanley's Backyard Fitness Center (the movement explorer is only part of the Fitness Center) write: The Stanley Works, Advertising Services, P.O. Box 1800, New Britain, Connecticut 06050.

Small outside exercise units can be made or purchased commercially. Note the variety of potential activities: climbing, sliding, crawling and jumping. (Courtesy Constructive Playthings Co.)

Explore Indoor Movement

Physical exercise has a place in the home, too. Small units such as these provide many opportunities for large muscle development. Both gym houses disassemble for compact storage. (Courtesy Creative Playthings Co. and American Plywood Association.)

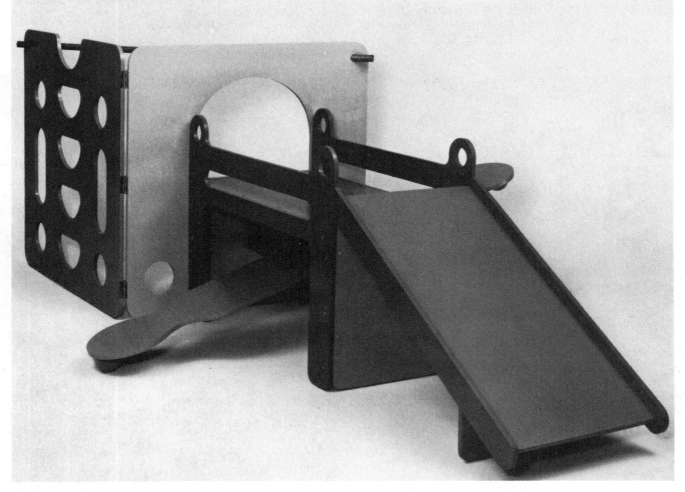

MOVING WITH SAFETY

Apparatus such as the movement explorer provide many opportunities for rolling, crawling, climbing, walking, jumping and balancing. Neuromuscularly and orthopedically handicapped children especially benefit from climbing, walking, balancing and crawling activities. These children as well as blind or partially sighted youngsters, who may fall while climbing, need soft cover under and around play equipment. For a partially sighted or a physically handicapped child, normally afraid to fall, launching out through space in the certainty of a soft landing is a liberating experience. Beyond fostering the sense of unrestricted movement and self-confidence, landing and bouncing on soft cover (an old mattress, for example) also helps the disabled child to better understand cause and effect as their bodies move.

"Children who are handicapped may have had limited physical experiences because of their disabilities, as well as problems with perception", write the planners and designers of New York City's *A Playground for All Children*. "Because of this, play involving a cause-effect relationship, and play which develops the child's awareness of his kinesthetic abilities is particularly needed. Soft materials and non-traditional materials such as vinyl and foam lend themselves particularly well to this type of play. The child, losing himself in play, develops a better knowledge of his body and what it can do. Additionally the lack of specific expectations in soft play permits the child to enjoy himself without fear of failure."

PULLEY GLIDE

If your yard is large enough, you may want to build the movement explorer some distance away from your treehouse (social and physical play

Pulley glides work the upper body, an area which usually doesn't get enough exercise from other equipment. (Courtesy Childcraft.)

Climbing nets, when hung loosely, will give kids first-hand experience into the dynamics of cause-and-effect.

don't always mix unless there is an imaginative link). A piece of exercise equipment that can be used to connect the two structures, providing lots of imaginative play potential for kids seven and up, is a pulley glide.

The glide can be any height or length, depending on the age of the children using it. The drop-off spot can be sand or any other soft material. A rise in the rope level just before reaching the drop-off area will help slow the child to a safe stop. The pulley glide, besides stimulating imagination and dramatic play, helps to exercise the upper body.

Use an industrial pulley with a sealed eye. The pulley fits over a ½" steel cable strung between the treehouse (or a 8" diameter post sunk four feet into the ground) and two 8" diameter posts sunk into the ground some distance away. These last two posts, located at the drop-off point, are joined by a crossbeam mounted at a height of seven feet from the ground. Connect the cable to the take-off post by driving large nails (at least 40d) or lag bolts into the timber. Leave enough of the nails or bolts protruding to hold up the cable which is looped around the tree or post. Secure the cable with a clamp. Now fasten the free end of the cable to the crossbeam at the landing site with a heavy-duty eye-bolt and clamp. Provide sand or other soft material for easy touch-downs.

A drop of ten feet over a distance of fifty feet is suggested for older children (ease the slope for the younger set). By regulating the tautness of the cable, you can assure that the pulley and its rider will slow down sufficiently for a soft landing.

NETS

Climbing nets also add considerably to the imaginative uses of a treehouse. A rope or cargo net (available from government surplus outlets) has lots of physical and developmental plusses because the scrambling and balancing involves many muscles. If the net is hung loosely, it's surface will change constantly with the distribution of children.

Climbing nets can be thrown over large saw horses or secured to the side of any nearby structure. A unique frame for these versatile nets also can be made from discarded trees. That's right, discarded trees! City recreation departments, departments of public works, and tree-service companies often clear trees from public lands. If you have room in your yard, you might ask one of these agencies for some of the limbs and trunks they've removed. Sink these trees in 3-5 foot holes filled with compacted soil (or cement if you want them to be permanent fixtures) and build yourself a maze of interconnecting skyways and nets. Bolt the branches together to give the maze rigidity. These reclaimed trees can be made even more interesting with the addition of platforms, knotted ropes for climbing as well as nets to jump into.

material that protects against falls but still provides good traction.

A playhouse firmly rooted in the ground, but one which gives young climbers a commanding view of their surroundings, has been created by the Canadian Children's Advisory Service. This structure, shown on page 30 is designed for the seven-and-under crowd, is built with safety foremost in mind. The stairs are a case in point.

Ladders, steps and stairs can be the downfall of children unless they are designed with safety in mind. When building stairs, make the spacing height between steps no greater than 14 inches if your kids are less than six years of age. For children seven and older, space steps anywhere from 14" to 18" apart. The angle of inclination on stairs and other climbing devices should permit children to stand vertically on one level without the lower portion of their legs contacting the next upper level.

Stair and platform protective railing should be cylindrical if handicapped children are to use the platform. The diameter of the railing should allow for a grip that does not allow encircling fingertips to touch the palm. Handrails can be steel cable wrapped in vinyl or painted steel pipe.

Slides can be another sore point, both for parents and kids. The large area at the top of this Canadian-designed playhouse assures greater safety by allowing for group waiting and queuing. Children who decide at the last moment to pass up a quick ride down the slide can make a graceful retreat without forcing their way back down a steep ladder.

To prevent kids from falling out or tipping over (particularly important for handicapped youngsters) add high sides and a reverse bend at the bottom of the slide to slow the final feet of descent.

An alternative to a stainless steel sliding surface is high-density polyethylene. Opaque in color, this inexpensive, lightweight plastic comes in various thicknesses and has a low coefficient of friction, making it an ideal surface for sliding. Secure the polyethylene to a plywood undersurface or underrunner with round head, self-tapping wood screws (#10, ¾").

According to the Canadian Children's Environments Advisory Service, playhouses generally should not be combined with climbing structures because strenuous physical play is in conflict with social play. However, physical apparatus can be used for imaginative, social interaction. The slide on the playhouse appears to conflict with social play, at first glance. But, actually it plays a subordinate role, as just a quick way down.

SAFETY

The sight of a cargo net or pulley glide may send some parents into a tizzy. Safety is certainly every parent's concern and "Will my child be safe playing on that piece of equipment?" is a legitimate question. But safety must be put into its proper perspective. Children are born risk-takers, and their bodies are resilient and geared for the risks of growing up. Most scrapes and sprains disappear before they're noticed.

Children need to take risks in order to discover their potential and their limitations. "How high can I climb?," "Where do I jump from here?," "Is it safe to go down this way?" are the questions children must often answer for themselves.

Risk and safety are not entirely incompatible. You can design safe exercise equipment: 1) Locate the structure away from interfering obstacles. Pulley glides, for example, should be placed where children will be discouraged from running through the pulley's path. 2) Scale the equipment to the child's size. 3) Use sturdy materials. 4) Be on the lookout for protruding bolts, nails and screws. 5) Round sharp corners and sand areas that are potential breeding grounds for splinters.

Ground cover is another way to plan for safety. Grass and medium-sized particles of tanbark are good substances. So is dirt until it gets wet and becomes mud. Sand softens landings, but provides little running traction. Outdoor carpeting is a great synthetic substance, but you'll probably spend a great deal of time securing it (ripples and lumps in the material increase the chances of falling and tripping). The ideal surface is a soft

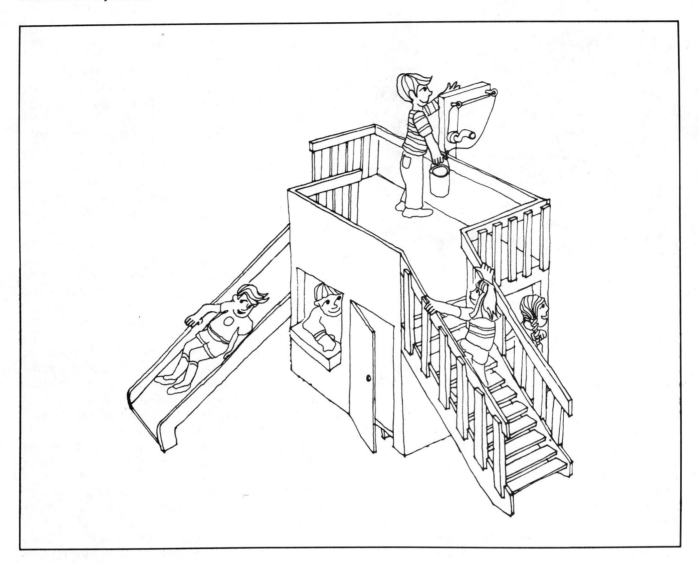

A Safe Playhouse for young Climbers

1. Playhouse dimensions: 5'0'' (1500 mm) wide x 7'0'' (2100 mm) long x 5'0'' (1500 mm) high.
2. Railing 2'0'' (600 mm) high with supports at 6'' (150 mm) centers.
3. Stainless steel slide 2'0'' (600 mm) wide x 10'0'' (150 mm) long. Lip of slide to be 4'' (100 mm) off grade.
4. Stairs 2'0'' (600 mm) wide; rise to be 5'' (125 mm), tread 8'' (200 mm).
5. ¾'' (19 mm) fir ply treated sides.
6. ¾'' (19 mm) fir ply floor inside.

(Courtesy of The Canadian Children's Environment Advisory Service)

Slide is embedded in an earth mound. Note safety feature for handicapped children: high sides and reverse bend to stop kids at bottom.

Slides for all sizes

Indoor treehouses make ideal, quiet retreats . . . but not if more than one kid's hanging around. Before you know it, everyone's perched on top.

Accessories such as the pulley should also be used to extend dramatic play rather than for physical exercise.

TREEHOUSE FURNITURE

Let the kids build their own furniture. They can do it without being master craftsmen. Everyday millions of people discard items that appear useless; but, when viewed through knowing eyes, these materials are ideal building supplies. Some of the nicest looking and longest-lasting playhouse furniture have been pieced together with discarded wooden boxes.

You needn't rummage around in the garbage piles, though, to find these gems. Ask a store owner if there are any packing materials he intends to throw away. Then offer to cart them away yourself, saving him time and labor. A great trade for everyone involved.

You can create just about anything you or your children can imagine from these leftover wooden crates, cardboard boxes, and fiberboard drums. They make excellent chairs, tables, beds, desks, book shelves, easels, stools, storage chests, couches, or partitions. The list is endless. Have you noticed any old peach or pear crates lying by the fruit bin of your local supermarket? With a few nails or screws and a bit of fresh paint, the kids can put together storage shelves for their treehouse.

INDOOR TREEHOUSES

Take a treehouse inside! Indoor treehouses offer the same sense of privacy and secrecy, of "being above it all". The indoor variety has often gone under the name of carrel, but any youngster will tell you it's really an indoor treehouse.

One of the nicest models I've run across was built by the teenage son of a nursery school owner. Constructed from easy-to-come-by materials, the Dan Malloney indoor treehouse breaks down in a few seconds and can be moved from room to room.

Construction of the Dan Malloney indoor treehouse requires a cross cut saw, hammer, hand drill, and wrenches for building details see pages 41 and 42.

For climbing: A jungle gym

Ideal for hard play. Even when a crowd of neighborhood children comes running, this structure can withstand the assault.

Start assembling: The post is set into the ground. A tenon has been cut at one end to which the two verticals are attached with threaded bolts and nuts. The tenon is of the same thickness as the vertical member.

The structure can be built of standard 2 x 6 or 2 x 8 lumber. If treated lumber is available, use it. Lumber treated with either pentachlorophenol (PCP) or Wolmanized is satisfactory. Creosoted material is not; it will dirty clothing. Even if you do not use treated material for the superstructure, it is important to use it for the foundation pieces.

Within a few hours, the entire structure can be prepared for erection.

Preliminary Work

The foundation posts should be about 36 in. long, notched to receive the uprights about 10 in. from the end. Use either 4 x 6 or 4 x 8 for these, depending on what you are using for the superstructure.

The eight pieces holding the verticals together, as ring beams, are notched 1¼ in. deep by 4½ in. wide to receive lumber (check lumber thickness), 6 in. from the ends. Drill the four pieces for the horizontal bars. Drill through the two inside pieces and halfway through the outer mem-

bers. These pieces also need to be notched for the piece that carries one end of the floor boards. These members are attached by lag screws between and inside of the verticals.

The other four are bolted together with blocking in between to form two crossbeams.

Into the ladder sides drill 1 in. holes 8 in. apart. Cut small wedges out of the ends of the rungs, about 1½ in. long, to form notches. Glue and nail the rungs into position and then drive somewhat larger wedges into the notches to lock the rungs into position.

If you are using untreated lumber, you may wish to brush on two coats of preservative at this point.

Erection

Connect the verticals to the foundation pieces, which are set about 24 in. into the ground. Of course, make sure that the foundation posts are level with each other.

At 6 ft. 6 in. height, attach the horizontal ring beams with lag screws. The notches must be to the out-

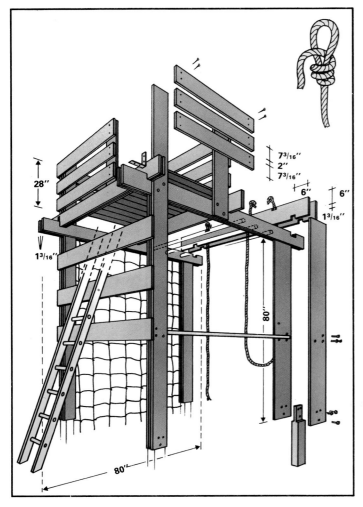

After one side has been assembled, the short posts for the railing and the railing boards can be screwed on.

side of the vertical pieces (see drawing).

The short posts for the railing and the railing itself are attached with screws. Assemble the other side the same way.

Use metal framing clips to attach the ring beams to each other. Screw or nail floor boards to the beams. Reinforce the post at the left of the railing with a piece of scrap lumber.

Fold net at the edges over strips which are inserted between verticals and secured with screws.

Attach lower horizontal bar with three carriage bolts at each end. Protruding ends of the bolts should be sawn off and filed smooth for safety.

The rope ends should have double knots (see drawing). Pull the rope end through the loop and tighten.

The ladder is stuck into the ground and fastened at the top to the protruding end of the ring beam with three screws.

Finish by fastening the three horizontal boards on the ladder side with screws.

This is the joint for the parallel beams: in a type of sandwich construction the vertical members are screwed to the horizontal boards. The parallel beam is held by an angle bracket attached with screws.

To give the structure added support, rocks are placed next to the posts. Fill the hole with dirt, water, and after a while tamp thoroughly.

To prevent climbing rope and swing from sliding, a notch is sawed into the parallel rails. Nail a piece of scrap lumber between the knots of the swing-rope to prevent it from pulling out.

The floor boards are nailed to a crossboard and the outer parallel rail. Countersink nails to prevent injuries!

The climbing structure is finished. The three boards on the ladder side are also for climbing, and help stabilize the structure.

Let your children in on the joys of homeownership. Our fort is solid and will be the pride and joy of any youngster. You will have a reason to be proud, too, because anyone who has built our playhouse has shown the ability to do some serious carpentry work.

The fort in the garden for little adventurers

To give you an idea of how big it is: this playhouse is 100 in. long and 78 in. wide. The inside room will be 81 in. high and the peak of the roof gable is 122 in. high. But don't let the size scare you; if you carefully study our illustrations and enjoy carpentry work, you should have no problems. Our sketch two pages over doesn't give any dimensions; we did that on purpose. This will give you the chance to build the house according to your need (number of children, space in your backyard). You can write your own dimensions on this sketch and order your material accordingly. Or use the materials list given, which indicates quantities that will enable you to build the size shown here.

First cut all the parts, then lay out all notches and overlaps as indicated in photo series. Cut in and chisel; work as precisely as possible. Avoid chiseling

away more than half the thickness of the material. Start assembling the pieces after preparing all the wood this way.

To be sure the fort can endure a storm, rest all four corners of the house on cement posts. Use premix concrete for this purpose. Embed anchor clips so you can attach the stilts. Pay attention so that your four corners are accurately placed, and check that your cornerposts are perfectly level with each other.

To put up the frame you will need helpers. Set and mount the first two corner studs of a narrow side so that they meet at right angles on the cement posts. Screw on the cross-braces, which will later carry the floor boards. Re-

peat that procedure for the other two studs and connect the two narrow sides. Now check again that everything is level; there is still time to correct your cement posts if they need it. Next, mount the upper cross-braces of the narrow sides. Follow by attaching the roof-supporting plates, which have already been notched out (picture 7). Screw from the top with long wood screws onto cross-studs. Build the support construction for window and door frames, using carriage bolts. Now put up the ridge beam (picture 6). Then, notch and nail on the roof rafters, which are 1½ in. x 2⅜ in. studs, to finish the rough construction. After that, take a little time to celebrate.

1. After the concrete is poured in dug-out holes (with anchors), the basic construction consisting of four corner studs and floor construction will be erected.

LIST OF MATERIALS

Studs (for stilts and frame): 4 x 4 x 125 ft.	Plywood panel: 120 sq. ft.
18 Rafters: 2 x 3 (or 2 x 4), 57″	Carriage bolts: 32½″ x 5″
Tongue-and-groove boards: 175 sq. ft.	Carriage bolts: 18½″ x 7″
	Carriage bolts: 4½″ x 8″

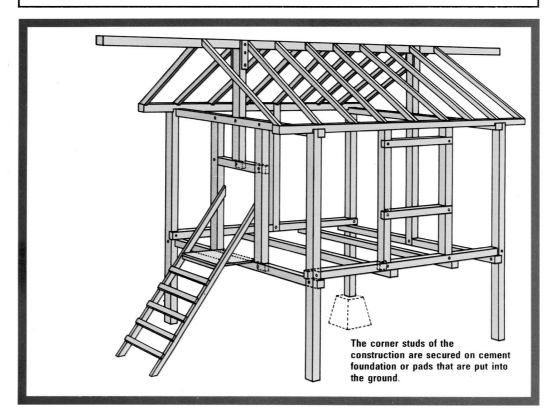

The corner studs of the construction are secured on cement foundation or pads that are put into the ground.

Installing the long floor boards in door opening. Screw a 1 x 4 underneath, so the ladder can be attached later.

3. Drill a ½" hole in all overlaps and use a 5" long carriage bolt to attach (our picture shows ridge support).

5. The next three pictures show assembly details. This is an overlap joint of the floor construction. For areas where studs have been notched out less than half of the material thickness, use 7"-long carriage bolts. Use washers with nuts and tighten well.

6. The supports holding the ridge are made of 1" boards. Three 7"-long carriage bolts are used for a solid connection. The upper end of boards are mitered.

7. The outer support plate is notched and screwed from the top onto the corner studs. Nail on the rafters, which also have to be notched.

4. When it comes to putting up the ridge beam, you will need a strong helper. The beam is put in the prepared supports.

8. The upper ends of the ladder are used as handrails. To outlast rough-playing kids, it should be screwed onto the vertical door studs. Nail on the platform. Important: Saw off all bolt ends! Danger of injury!

9. Doors and window shutters are built of tongue-and-grooved boards. Cut curves with a sabre saw; nail on boards.

10. For the final outside paneling, tongue-and-grooved boards are used again. These boards are put together in their tongue-in-grooves, and nailed onto studs on a 40° angle.

Pictures 9-11 illustrate how to build the doors and window shutters as well as how to finish the walls with grooved boards. The roof will be covered with plywood panels that are nailed on. Weatherproof your construction by applying a primer. As the final touch, apply an oil base lacquer. Note the over-hanging ridge beam, which is very handy for a climbing rope or a rope ladder.

11. Cover roof with four sheets of plywood. Clamp each sheet first, then nail on.

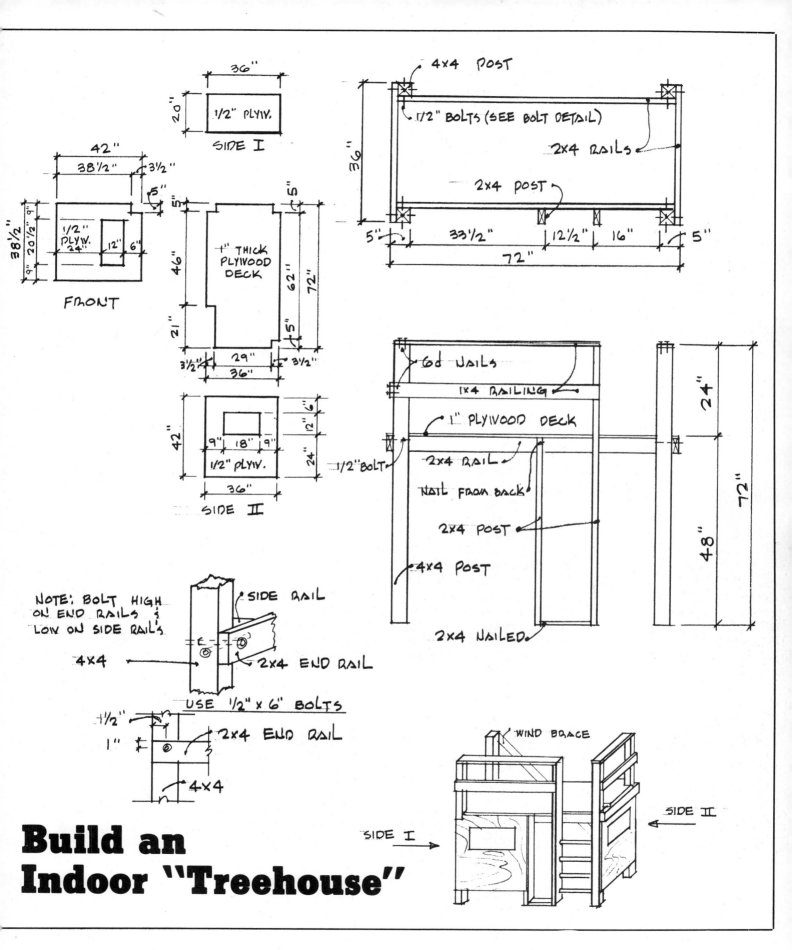

36"
20"
1/2" PLYW.
SIDE I

42"
38 1/2"
3 1/2"
5"
5"
1/2" PLYW.
9"
20 1/2"
38 1/2"
9"
24"
12"
6"
FRONT

4×4 POST
1/2" BOLTS (SEE BOLT DETAIL)
2×4 RAILS
2×4 POST
36
5"
33 1/2"
12 1/2"
16"
5"
72"

5"
5"
1" THICK PLYWOOD DECK
46"
62"
72"
21"
3 1/2"
29"
3 1/2"
36"

6d NAILS
1×4 RAILING
1" PLYWOOD DECK
2×4 RAIL
NAIL FROM BACK
2×4 POST
4×4 POST
2×4 NAILED

24"
72"
48"

6"
12"
42"
9"
18"
9"
1/2" PLYW.
24"
36"
SIDE II
1/2" BOLT

NOTE: BOLT HIGH ON END RAILS & LOW ON SIDE RAILS
SIDE RAIL
4×4
2×4 END RAIL
USE 1/2" × 6" BOLTS

1/2"
1"
2×4 END RAIL
4×4

WIND BRACE
SIDE I
SIDE II

Build an Indoor "Treehouse"

MATERIALS YOU'LL NEED

Frame
4 6'x4''x4''
3 6'x2''x4''
2 3'x2''x4''
1 4'x2''x4''
1 12½''x2''x4''

Railing
2 54''x1''x4''
3 3'x1''x4''

Top
1 3'x6'x1'' plywood

Front
1 42''x39''x½'' plywood

Side I
1 36''x20''x½'' plywood

Side II
1 36''x42''x½'' plywood

Steps
4 1''D. dowels 16'' long

Miscellaneous
8 ½'' bolts 6'' long
Common nails (4d [1½''] and 10d [3''])

Optional back brace
1 8'x4'' x 1''x4''

Build the frame first. Secure each main corner with two bolts (all other joints can be nailed). Use a 1'' auger bit to drill holes for the dowel steps. Insert the steps while building the frame. Cut and fit sides and top after the frame is complete. You now have the perfect addition to any playroom or bedroom.

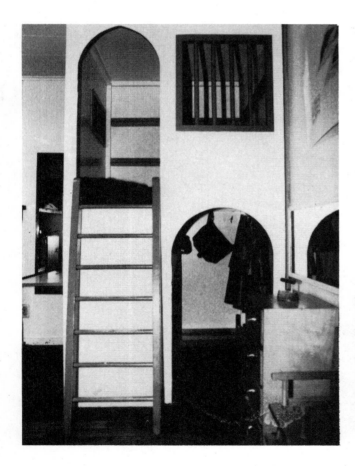 

Indoor treehouses can help you effectively manage the space in a playroom. In both treehouses, the upper platform is for quiet or social play. The lower space in the treehouse on the left is used to store hats, coats and boots. The area under the play structure on the right is reserved for reading and quiet talking.

Low branching trees create spaces that become natural treehouses.

Shrubs, potted or in the ground, add to the beauty and natural gaiety of children's play spaces.

LIVING TREEHOUSES

Rudolf Doernach, a German architect, thinks natural treehouses might be the next step in family homes. Doernach (a good name for an architect) believes it's silly to wait 80 years for a tree to grow, then chop it down for lumber. "Killing a tree to make a house is easy," he observes, "but is it intelligent?".

At Doernach's Biotecture Institute near Stuttgart, the architect has a "house farm" where he practices "agrotecture". Simply stated, Doernach trains growing trees and trims them into experimental houses. To build one of his natural treehouses, wire together the upper branches of two or more trees, then cover them with a netting that shapes the roofline. Vines and other plants fill out the walls. For door and window openings, whack away with the clippers. Put up interior nets filled with insulating materials that seal the roof and walls. Doernach suggests laying a floor of foam blocks and then installing plumbing, wiring, and partitions.

Doernach's treehouses are many years away, but natural treehouses for your children already may be sitting in the front or backyard.

Trees that branch to the ground make excellent natural tents and hideouts for children of all ages. With the addition of props, these spaces become the backdrop for hours of dramatic play. Among the conifers, Port Orford cedar and lassen cypress are excellent. Other trees that make fine, natural playhouses include the weeping mulberry, camper down elm, and weeping willow. Pine trees, which are not conducive to climbing and treehouse building because of their sticky pitch, make excellent ground houses, most coming furnished with a carpet of soft needles.

Any large shrub (8'—12") with a branching habit giving way to open space under the limbs also makes a fine, cozy nook and resting area for children. You can acquire landscaping plants and shrubs for free or from park and recreation departments, departments of public works or tree-service companies at a low cost. With the addition of kid-sized tables, chairs, crates and planks, these natural spaces can become the site for hours of fun-filled social and dramatic play.

If your backyard is too small for this forest of shrubbery, take matters into your own hands and create a garden of natural treehouses on your concrete patio. You will need a little soil, several planter boxes and a green thumb. Tub plants (geraniums, tulips, daffodils, fuchsias, and English lavender) can be arranged into little hideaways and private retreats on most patios and porches.

Planter boxes, with casters attached for mobility, are easy to build and provide homes for many different varieties of shrubs. With sturdy bushes planted in one or more of these movable planters, your kids can design and make their own hideouts or small, outdoor rooms for quiet or social play. Tub flowers add visual gaiety to play areas. Plants and shrubs also provide animal cover. They attract birds, butterflies, and creepy-crawlers and create a good environment for showing children the marvels of the natural world.

The shade offered by these living treehouses and mazes during warm weather provides a pleasant way to keep cool. Shade is particularly important for many disabled children. Mentally retarded and brain damaged children as well as those with chronic conditions such as heart disease, diabetes, epilepsy and hemophilia or with neuromuscular and orthopedic handicaps almost always require special consideration. Since drinking may be a difficult problem for some of these kids, authorities believe that dehydration may be a serious consequence of active, outdoor play. Some medications also interfere with the normal perspiration process and other drugs may cause sun-sensitivity. This can lead to overheating. A shady, living treehouse offers a practical solution.

ADVENTURE GARDENS

Gardening has long been an activity for learning and emotional satisfaction. Children of all ages and temperaments are intrigued by the process of growth. With a bit of imagination, you can turn the family garden into an emotionally satisfying and adventurous play area for your children.

An adventure garden incorporates simple structures like raised beds and bean tents and tunnels, with growing plots laid out in irregular form. According to Russell Beatty of the Department of Landscape Architecture at the University of California in Berkeley, the garden plants most often selected are common edible vegetables such as carrots, chard, or tomatoes; and enormous or unusual plants such as sunflowers, spaghetti squash, or giant pumpkins. "The intent of an adventure garden," Beatty explains, "is to allow children to experience the excitement of growing plants of interest to them in the creative atmosphere of a playground."

Corn can be grown in confusing mazes. Beans can be grown on string frames, creating tunnels and leafy, enclosed spaces. Use your imagination

and test out any theories or ideas your family may have.

From his experience with adventure gardens, Beatty has learned that children need to feel personally involved in their creation and operation. Through this involvement, tremendous enthusiasm emerges. If the kids feel that the garden is their place, they tend to develop a keen sense of responsibility towards the growing plants.

"As a learning experience, a multitude of skills beyond those involved in gardening are possible," according to Beatty. "Art can be experienced in the sketching of a flower; arithmetic in the counting of seeds or the measuring of plots; music in the singing of songs about gardens; science in the miracle of growth and decay; and, literature in the poetry of the garden. Discipline is quickly learned when plants die from lack of care. Cooperation can result when the children share their experiences or help tend each other's plots. Culture and history can be learned from the use of the gourd as a ladle, the symbolic celebration of an Indian feast, or the creation of corn husk dolls like those made by the pioneers."

Beatty points out that gardens are not limited solely to single families. Dead spaces in housing developments can become focal points of activity for entire neighborhoods with community gardens.

For best results, divide your adventure garden into irregularly spaced plots 2½' wide by 6' long. This area gives younger children maximum frontage with a minimum need to step into the planted areas.

Once the garden has come to maturity and the bean tunnels and corn mazes are ready for harvest, you can prepare a feast in a banquet hall right out of *Jack and the Beanstalk.* You'll need some string and several handfuls of sunflower seeds. In the spring lay out the boundary for the living sunflower walls, then dig up the soil around the border. Go down at least 12" and fertilize well. Plant the sunflower seeds ¾" deep, about 3" apart. When you notice the tiny sprouts poking their heads several inches above the ground, thin the plants to one every 8"-10" (for extra strong walls, plant double rows). When the yellow giants have grown to a towering five feet, tie the tops of the two opposing walls together to form a roof. The result is a banquet hall fit for anyone's harvest feast!

Once the dishes have been scraped clean, the remaining greens composted, and the sunflowers cut and hung up to dry, gather the whole family together and plan ahead for next year's adventure.

2
Dollhouses

Deke, our 2½-year-old, loves to play with miniatures of people, cars, food, animals, and furniture. He sits for hours in his special play corner in the living room and recreates life and the world as he sees it. He plans picnics to the beach and airplane rides over San Francisco Bay. He designs zoos and, on occasion, stages car races and spectacular crashes. I often sit for long stretches of time, fascinated by my young son's

Starting with only the basic cardboard frame, this dollhouse becomes the beginning of unlimited creativity, for most any child.

exploits. The miniatures are perfect vehicles for acting out his fantasies.

Small duplicates of real-life objects have the same magical hold on older children. Dollhouses, in turn, add an extra dimension to miniature play. When my young son's cars crash, he often sends the wreckage back to their house to "get better". Play with dollhouses also provides ample opportunity for social play with peers. Dollhouses give children a sense of power and superiority that is hard to come by in a world of big grown-ups. In short, dollhouses and the miniatures that accompany them provide children, boys and girls, with avenues for creativity and social play in a non-threatening environment.

Miniature houses range from the humble to the magnificent. You and your kids can throw them together for a few cents or you can spend thousands of dollars on a single house and a few original pieces of furniture. The expensive variety, though, are more likely to be collector's items and are better kept out of the reach of children of all ages. If collecting dollhouses is your hobby this chapter isn't for you. But if you're thinking about building a dollhouse for your active youngsters to play with then read on for a number of exciting possibilities.

CARDBOARD DOLLHOUSE

The dollhouse and furniture pictured on page 46 were built entirely out of cardboard boxes, construction paper, matchboxes, popsicle sticks and an untold number of "left-overs". The house was the project of a small suburban library located in El Sobrante, California. Over the course of an exciting week, 25 kids, ranging in age from three to eleven, built and furnished the dollhouse under the supervision of the Children's Librarian.

A dab of paint, paper shingles, miniature trees and a slide can transform the plainest of cardboard boxes into a well-landscaped, attractive dollhouse.

Build a "Creative" Cardboard Dollhouse

Cardboard dollhouses can be furnished to the hilt with elegant furniture made from bottle caps, thimbles, empty tape dispensers, pieces of sponge and match boxes. Working with "leftovers" to furnish a dollhouse fosters imagination and creativity in children.

Here is a list of some of the materials that went into the dollhouse project: a discarded cardboard box provided the basic frame for the dollhouse; clear plastic fitted over cutouts in the cardboard became windows; roof shingles were cut out of brown construction paper; the evergreens on the front lawn were made out of green crepe paper; strips of cardboard and construction paper were transformed into stairs; a toilet paper tube was made into a fireplace and chimney; pieces of sponge and styrofoam were shaped into furniture; an empty strawberry basket became a play pen; a plastic tape dispenser was transfigured into a toilet bowl. The dollhouse was completed with touches of fresh paint for the outside wood paneling, and the bricks in the chimney. It will never be completely furnished because children will always think of something else to add. Matchboxes become storage closets and tongue depressors, laced together with string, picket fences. Bottle caps become stepping stones around the side of the house or cereal bowls for the breakfast table and small scraps of wood are turned into appliances with the addition of a little paint. Pieces of cloth are transformed into wall-to-wall carpets, and Christmas wrapping paper graces the interior cardboard becoming fancy wallpaper.

Obviously, the variations on this "potluck" dollhouse are many. Substitute a wooden crate for the cardboard box and the life expectancy of the miniature increases by many years. Add a cardboard or wooden crate garage and barn, and the house becomes a small country estate. The only rule for constructing dollhouses and their furnishings is to follow the dictates of your children's imaginations.

In addition to furniture, dollhouses need people to occupy them. Younger kids can make their own dolls with a wire coathanger and multi-colored beads. You can help them shape the coat-hanger into the form of a person, then let them add the beads in any order they please. Once the last bead has slid into position, lock them into place by bending the end of the wire into a tight loop.

Instead of coat-hangers, you may find it easier for your children to work with pipe cleaners. Pipe cleaner people can be shaped easily into any number of positions by young children. The cost of pipe cleaner people is minimal, therefore broken or damaged limbs can be mended inexpensively.

Another dollhouse constructed from heavy, corrugated cardboard (or from ½" plywood if you want greater durability) is pictured below. For the cardboard versions, glue and masking tape will hold most of the joints together satisfactorily. If you decide to use plywood, stick with the white glue, but pound in at least three finishing nails at each of the major joints to insure stability.

The dollhouse below, originally designed and built by the parents of Sierra Madre Community Nursery School in Sierra Madre, California, can be

The "Sierra Madre"

Dollhouses, by allowing children to project their fantasies onto inanimate objects, help youngsters work out their understanding of the world in a nonthreatening environment. (Courtesy Sierra Madre Community Nursery School)

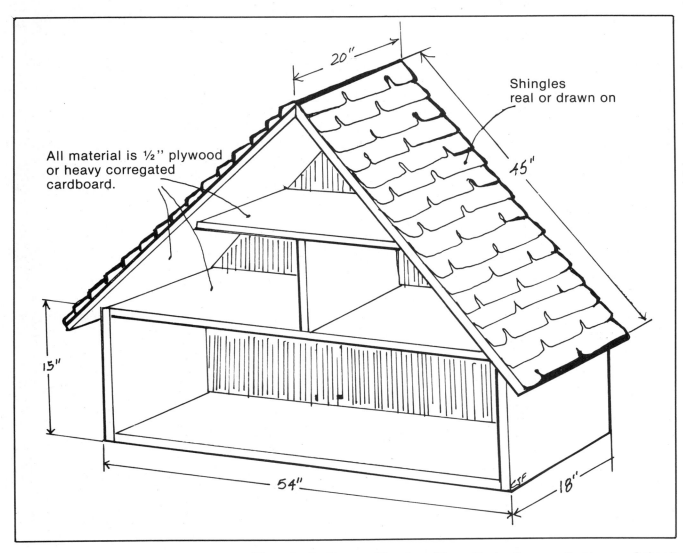

20"

Shingles
real or drawn on

45"

All material is ½" plywood
or heavy corregated
cardboard.

15"

54"

18"

Plans for Dollhouse. (Courtesy Sierra Madre Community Nursery School)

outfitted in the same manner described above. Your children also might add some cardboard furniture of their own design. The procedure is simple. You cut out two identical profiles with one or more sandwiched-in pieces. A chair, for example, consists of two identical, parallel sides with a seat and a back glued in between. For a cupboard, chest of drawers or vanity, the kids will need to join together the two parallel sides with a top, bottom, and back piece.

The youngsters can make many of these same pieces of cardboard furniture without glue or tape. All they'll need is a pair of scissors and several empty milk cartons. Turn the milk carton upside down. Imagine that the bottom of the carton is the top of a table. Now have the kids sketch the side of the table and the four legs on the sides of the carton (the table's legs are formed by the carton's edges). Cut along the pattern and have a perfect table to add to any dollhouse.

Make a chair by cutting out the seat and legs in the same manner. To make the arms and back, your youngsters can cut a wide band from the unused center of the carton. Push the lower edge of this band down over the seat. It's easier to do if the kids carefully fit the band over three corners first and then pull it over the fourth corner. Trim the band to make back and arm rests.

MODULAR DOLLHOUSE

Modular construction is one way to build a dollhouse that can be expanded as your children grow older. Except for the pyramid shaped attic, the dollhouse pictured below is made from identical rectangular sections stacked on top of each other. Literally, the sky is the limit with this miniature house. As it climbs steadily towards the center beam of your roof, it's advisable to brace the dollhouse along the sides or in the back so that it doesn't accidentally topple over on a child. Eyelets at the top and bottom of each section will allow a wooden dowel to pass through and hold modules securely together. When the kids want to dismantle their modular dollhouse, all they need to do is remove the dowel.

Fill this dollhouse with traditional Scandinavian toy people and animals. To make the people, give your children small, firm, golden stalks of wheat or rye. They also need twine to hold the straw shafts in place and a pair of scissors. The straw creations may require some stitching to get the different body parts to stay in place, so have sewing thread and needle nearby. Depending on the thickness of the straw you use, it may be necessary to soak the shafts in water to make them more flexible.

When all is ready, begin by folding a handful of straw in half. With the bent middle portion sticking up, tie off one section with twine to form the head. Use several more lengths of twine to tie off the main body and the doll's legs. Rather than tying off the legs of a traditional lady doll, trim the

Modular dollhouses have the added advantage of being able to grow with your children, and their imagination!

Dollhouses fashioned from pegboard can be laced together with yarn or twine. Add yarn handles to make the house portable.

ends of the straw to form a full-length skirt. Insert several more lengths of straw just below the neck to make the arms, then tie the straw in sections to form the elbows and wrists. Smaller bunches of straw can be added for hair. Buttons make wonderful eyes and noses. Stitch on a bright red mouth or use cloth to add a smile to the doll's face. With the same basic technique, you can create a variety of animals including cows, horses, dogs, birds and even goldfish!

PEGBOARD

Cardboard and plywood are sturdy materials for constructing dollhouses. But they certainly aren't the only readily available building materials. Pegboard is another material that lends itself quite well to dollhouses and the developmental needs of younger children. Young kids are constantly learning new motor skills. Many of these skills involve hand/eye coordination. Dollhouses made from pegboard can encourage children to practice and improve their motor skills.

The holes in pegboard literally cry out to be filled. One idea is to fill the holes with colored yarn or twine, thereby decorating the dollhouse at the same time. The arrangement of the holes allows for a large variety of patterns. In fact, using pegboard and twine is an effective way to teach children basic geometric shapes.

Pegboard can be cut into different shapes such as squares, triangles or rectangles and used as the basic components for building modular dollhouses. By lacing together walls, roofs, and floor parts, children can build their own dollhouses. And

when the mood strikes they can "tear down" their creations by simply removing the thread, leaving all the parts intact for the next structure.

Pegboard lends itself to additional creative uses. Hinges for doors and folding roofs are quickly made from yarn laced through adjacent holes. The pegboard dollhouse can be made portable with the addition of yarn straps. Manufacture furniture from pre-cut pieces, lace together with twine, and then set upright on legs made from nuts and bolts.

ENGLISH BUNGALOW

Harlan Barr, a master craftsman working in Oakland, California, designs and builds children's toys. His speciality is dollhouses. Harlan uses 3/8" particleboard and secures all joints with white glue and finishing nails. His dollhouses are practically indestructible. To prove their durability, Harlan will gladly jump up and down on the dollhouse's roof, a feat that causes the average dollhouse to collapse. However, the Harlan dollhouse remains intact.

The English bungalow shown on page 51 is an excellent example of a sturdy, well-designed miniature. The house is modeled after a turn-of-the-century bungalow and possesses all the grace of a fine, older home. Yet it will withstand the onslaught of generations of children, making a great "hand-me-down" for any family. Harlan designed this dollhouse expressly for *Successful Playhouses.* You will need the following tools: hammer, measuring tape, cross-cut saw, carpenter's square, keyhole saw, drill, screw driver.

Build an English Bungalow

This miniature bungalow, made with particleboard, is designed to last for years. The gable roof can be raised and locked into place with friction lid supports. The side walls are easily removed, giving access to the first floor rooms.

MATERIALS

15'	¾''x2'' pine
4'x4'	⅛'' hardboard
4'x8'	⅜'' particleboard
3'3''	1''x1'' pine
5½'	¼''x¾'' stripping
1 lb.	¾'' finishing nails
	carpenter's glue
2	cabinet hinges
1	friction lid support

GENERAL INSTRUCTIONS

1. Cut and decorate all pieces before assembly.

2. Build from the bottom up.

3. Fasten all permanent joints with ¾'' finishing nails and white carpenter's glue (you'll need about a one pound box of nails to do the entire house).

4. Use a table saw to insure right angle cuts. If you don't have a table saw, take your materials to a woodworking shop and have them cut the wood to the proper dimensions.

BUILDING THE FLOOR FRAME

1. Assemble the floor frame from ¾''x2'' pine (A, A₁; B, B₁; C).

2. Cover the outside of the floor frame with ⅛'' hardboard (E, E₁; D, D₁).

3. The floor (F) is cut from ⅛'' hardboard. Starting from the rear of the hardboard floor on both sides, cut out a $\frac{7}{16}$'' x 24 ¾'' strip. Widen the last inch of each strip to 1'' square (the corner posts will rest in these 1'' square notches).

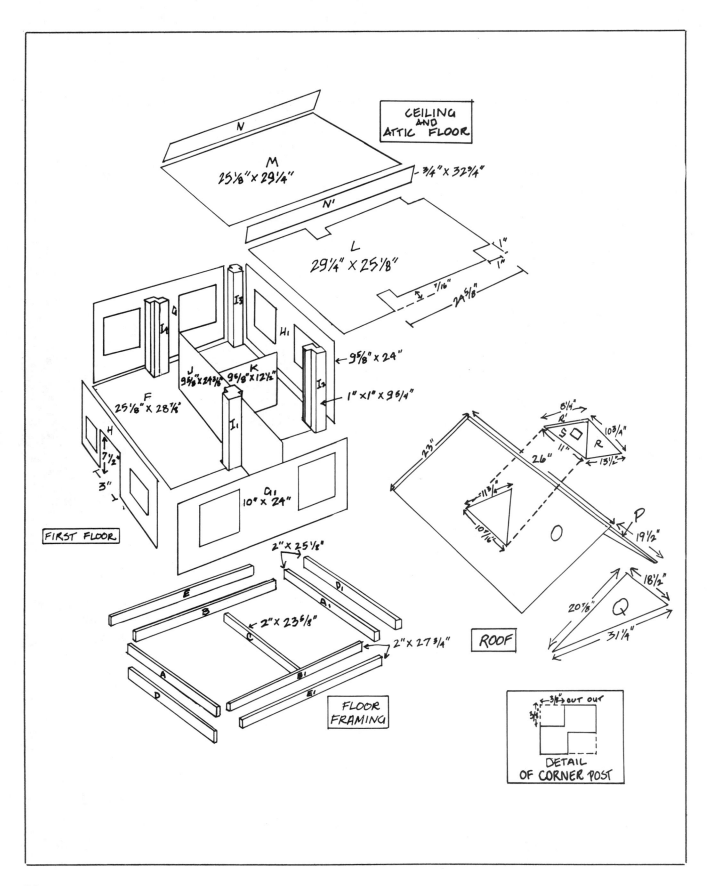

CEILING
AND
ATTIC FLOOR

N

M
25⅛" X 29¼"

¾" X 32¾"

N'

L
29¼" X 25⅛"

1"
1"

⁷⁄₁₆"
24⅝"

I₃

Q

I₄

H₁

9⅝" X 24"

J
9⅝"X24³⁄₈"

K
9⅝"X12½"

F
25⅛" X 28⅞"

I₂

1"X1"X9⅝"

I₁

H

7½"

T

3"

Y

C₁
10" X 24"

FIRST FLOOR

8¼"
R'
S
10¾"
R
11"
13½"

23"

26"

11¾"

P

10⅞"

19½"

10⁷⁄₁₆"

18½"

20⅞"

Q

31¼"

ROOF

2" X 25⅛"

E

D₁

B

A₁

2" X 23⅝"

C

A

B₁

D

E₁

2" X 27¾"

FLOOR
FRAMING

⅜" OUT OUT
¾"

DETAIL
OF CORNER POST

WALL ASSEMBLY

1. Cut the two side walls (G, G₁), the front (H), back (H₁), the center dividing wall (J) and the bedroom wall divider (K) from ⅜'' particleboard.

2. Cut a ⅛'' deep, ⅜'' wide dado down the center of "J" to accommodate "K."

3. Hundreds of different commercial playhouse windows and doors are available. Before you cut the window openings, find out what is available locally. Window holes are cut out by first drilling a hole in each of the window's four corners large enough to accept a keyhole saw.

4. Glue and nail the four corner posts (I, I₂, I₃, I₄) into place. The posts are cut from 1'' square lengths of pine. Be sure to cut out two ⅜'' square strips the length of each post. These strips are removed from diagonally opposite corners. See the plans for proper positioning of the posts in the floor frame.

CEILING AND ATTIC FLOOR

1. The ceiling (L) is cut from ⅜'' particle board.

2. Cut out strips in "L" identical to those you cut in "F."

3. Glue and nail "L" to the walls. Be sure each of the corner posts fits into the corner notches in "L."

4. Glue and nail the attic floor (M) into place. The floor is ⅛'' hardboard.

ROOF ASSEMBLY

1. The gable roof (O and P) also is made from ⅜'' particleboard. Cut an opening in "O" to accommodate the window housing.

2. Nail the roof onto the attic walls (Q, Q₁). Be sure that the larger roof segment (O) is facing the front of the bungalow.

3. The gable roof is attached to the rear of "M" with cabinet hinges.

4. Nail two ¼''x¾'' strips (N, N₁) to the side wall edges of the attic floor. When the roof is "closed," these strips will hold it securely in place.

PORCH

1. Add a porch railing and stairs to the front floor frame. You can buy porch railing in kit form or make one yourself.

The bungalow's roof can be raised and locked in place with friction lid supports attached to both rear corner posts of the attic floor. The raised roof gives access to the attic. The first floor of the house, in turn, is accessible from the two side walls. These walls (G, G₁) can be lifted out of place quite easily by simply pulling them up and out. When replacing, be sure that your kids put the walls in the tracks formed by the corner post notches before pushing into place.

With a sharp mat knife, older children can add finishing touches to this bungalow quite painlessly. For interior moldings, an ideal material is balsa wood. All craft and hobby stores carry this versatile wood (it takes paint or stain quite well and is light and easy to glue in place). A dozen ⅜'' square strips of balsa, about 20'' long, can be put to good use as molding in Harlan's bungalow. Interior moldings made especially for dollhouses can be purchased, but these are considerably more expensive than their balsa wood counterparts. The kids should do as much of the interior decorating as they can before you help them assemble the house. This pre-assembly work includes painting ceilings, walls and floors; papering; and putting in doors and windows. Painting the ceiling of the first floor is a back-breaking, eye-straining task if you wait until after the dollhouse is put together.

Every turn-of-the-century bungalow needs a shingle roof. The easiest way to shingle your dollhouse is to first paint the roof a color that goes well with the rest of the house. Once the paint has dried, use a felt-tipped pen to draw in the shingles. Balsa wood strips cut to size, or individual pine cone scales also make excellent shingles. Harlan recommends tongue depressors or popsicle sticks trimmed to size, then glued in place.

Your English bungalow can be expanded with little problem. Simply add a second and possibly third floor using these same plans and instructions. The porch area can become a balcony or it can be eliminated on upper floors. Add several commercially available bay windows and your multi-storied bungalow is transformed into an elegant Victorian structure.

Persons interested in learning more about this English bungalow, or about dollhouses in general, can write directly to Harlan Barr at 5299 College Ave., Oakland, California 94618.

BUNGALOW FURNITURE

Regardless of how many extra rooms you add, this cozy bungalow remains on a 1" to 1' scale. This is an ideal size because most commercially available dollhouse furniture is build on the same scale. Of course, the dollhouse builders in your family can make their own furniture. Mahogany and other more expensive varieties of wood can be had quite inexpensively, or for free, if you have access to shipping yards. Many imports enter this country in crates made from strips of these precious woods. Most of the time, the empty crates are broken up and discarded unless you get to the dock first. Closer to home, keep your eyes peeled for those large dumpsters contractors fill to the brim with wood scraps at construction sites. The contents of one of these dumpsters can supply your kids with enough building materials to furnish hundreds of dollhouses.

With careful attention to detail and a bit of patience, realistic period furniture can be made. Glance through old Sears and Roebuck catalogs in your nearest library to get ideas for different designs. Once you do begin to build, remember that accuracy is important. Check and double check all measurements before you cut.

Let your "mastercrafts children" practice their building skills on a turn-of-the-century folding screen. Take a length of construction paper and fold it two or three times (accordion-fashion). Cut the tops of the folded panels into peaks, cut legs at the bottom, and remove the inside areas to create a frame. Or, if you wish, make the framework for this screen out of balsa wood. Cut and glue scenes from gift wrapping paper, calendars or old cards, behind the cutout areas. The result will be a folding screen elegant enough to grace the living room of the finest dollhouse.

Another method to build furniture and decorations for your bungalow, and one that's fun for all members of the family, is to fashion the pieces from clay. For an extremely plastic clay that hardens without baking, heat 1 cup of salt in ⅓ cup water. Stir the mixture well until the brine begins

to bubble. Remove from the stove and stir in ½ cup cornstarch that has dissolved in ⅓ cup water. Once the sticky mixture is blended, knead by hand until smooth.

Let the children do as much of the work as possible. Besides being a fine lesson in chemistry, kneading is an excellent way for kids to displace stored-up energies and any feelings of aggression that might have accumulated during the day.

Mold the home-brewed clay into chairs, sofas, desks, beds, bowls, light fixtures, and kitchen appliances. Set the moist miniatures aside and allow them to dry in their own good time. Add paint for an extra touch of realism. With a steady hand, you and your offspring can create your own clay people to populate the bungalow.

COLONIAL DOLLHOUSE

Another historically fascinating dollhouse has been designed by the Stanley Tool Works. Their Colonial dollhouse is based on an actual house built in the 1776 period in New England. The original house is still standing. According to Edward Benfield, Manager of Public Information at Stanley, the interior plan of colonial homes was significantly different from modern homes. Families were big and had many bedrooms, but few clothes closets because they didn't own many clothes. And, of course, there were no bathrooms since indoor plumbing did not come into general use until late in the Nineteenth Centure. Fireplaces were an essential part of every room because central heating had not yet come into existence. Cooking was done over the open fire in the kitchen-keeping room. Early American settlers also used this keeping room as a refuge from hostile Indians and wild animals. Later on, the keeping room became the most important room in the house where the entire family would gather for meals, warmth, and companionship.

At one end of the keeping room was a large pantry or larder. At the other end was a "borning room", a snug place in which mothers gave birth. Later, the baby stayed there to be close to the warmth of the fire and near the mother who would be busy with household chores.

On the third floor or attic there often was a smoke oven for smoking hams, sides of bacon, and game. Hickory bark or corncobs were burned in the oven to provide the smoke.

This colonial dollhouse is an exact replica of an actual house built during the "1776" period in New England. (Courtesy The Stanley Works, Inc.)

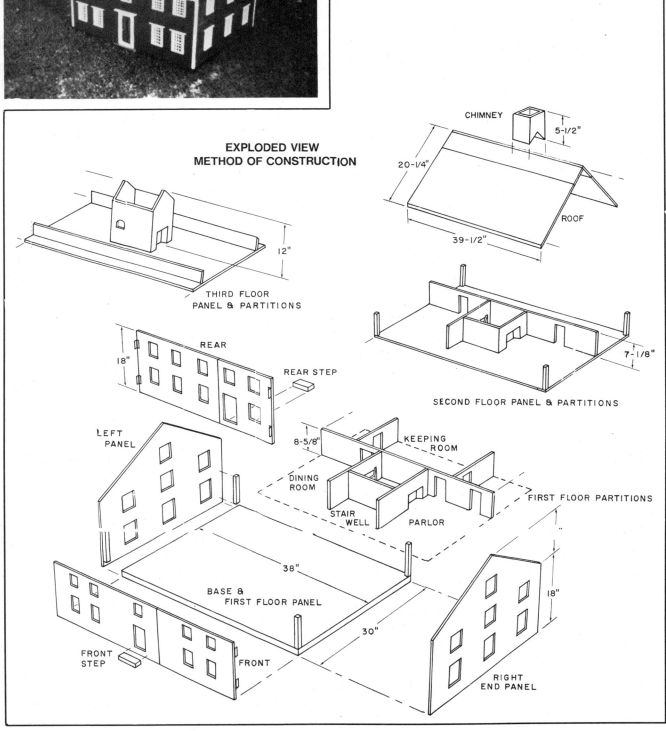

**EXPLODED VIEW
METHOD OF CONSTRUCTION**

CHIMNEY

5-1/2"

20-1/4"

ROOF

39-1/2"

THIRD FLOOR
PANEL & PARTITIONS

12"

7-1/8"

SECOND FLOOR PANEL & PARTITIONS

REAR

18"

REAR STEP

LEFT
PANEL

KEEPING
ROOM

8-5/8"

DINING
ROOM

FIRST FLOOR PARTITIONS

STAIR
WELL

PARLOR

38"

BASE &
FIRST FLOOR PANEL

18"

30"

FRONT
STEP

FRONT

RIGHT
END PANEL

MATERIALS

3 sheets 4'x8'x⅜" plywood (two sides good)
18' 1x"x2 for base and blocking
7" 1"x1" for corner posts, front and back steps
6 flathead screws 1¼" No. 10 for end panels
1 box of No. 18-1" long brads
1 box of No. 18-¾" long brads
1 box of No.18-½" long brads (for trim)
Carpenter's white glue
Hinges: 6—¾" x ⅝" for roof; 4—¾" x ⅝" for front and back door; 8—1½" x ⅞" for front and rear panels.

GENERAL INSTRUCTIONS FOR ASSEMBLING

First, build the base and then add the two end panels. Next, install the first floor partition, then add the second floor along with its partitions, and stairs from first to second floor. Install the third floor and its partitions and stairs. Add the front and rear panels. Add the fixed roof section, then the moveable sections of roof, and finally the chimney. Siding and roofing are last.

To insure a perfect match of identical elements (base panels, floor panels, end panels, front and rear panels, and moveable section of roof) clamp the pieces together and cut both at the same time. If you're going to install wooden windows, openings for them must be cut accurately to insure a perfect fit.

Because of restricted access, complete each floor (painting, paneling, trim, wallpaper, etc.) before proceding with the next floor. Apply wallpaper before installing interior trim. Paint all interior and exterior trim and elements for windows before cutting to size. Use glue and ½" brads to apply the trim.

Besides the furnishings already described in this chapter, you can outfit this Colonial with scraps of felt or plastic for floor coverings; cut pictures from magazines or Christmas cards and frame them with brass curtain rings or strips of balsa wood; make cupboards from matchboxes and flower pots from toothpaste tube tops; convert detergent bottle caps into wash tubs and flower pots; glue together two or three matchboxes for a large fireplace; stock the kitchen with food containers fashioned from pill jars; and decorate the walls with ornaments from broken jewelry.

A more detailed set of plans for the Colonial dollhouse may be obtained inexpensively by writing to: Stanley Advertising Services, The Stanley Works, P.O. Box 1800, New Britain, Connecticut 06050.

Additional ideas for dollhouse design and furnishings can be found in a catalog distributed by Federal Small Wares Corporation. You can receive their catalog free by writing to: Federal Small Wares, 85 Fifth Avenue, New York, New York 10003. Additional catalogs, can be obtained by writing to the following addresses (be sure to enclose a self-addressed, stamped envelope for prices):

The Miniature Catalog
Boynton & Associates
Clifton House
Clifton, VA 22024

AMSI Miniatures Catalog
P.O. Box 3497
San Rafael, CA 94902

For the true enthusiast, N.A.M.E. (National Association of Miniature Enthusiasts) offers several publications that are chock full of ideas and plans for the collector. Write to N.A.M.E., P.O. Box 2621, Brookhurst Center, Anaheim, CA 92804.

PAPER DOLLHOUSES

Dollhouses don't have to be made solely from cardboard and wood to be fun. With a bit of paper-folding magic, you and your children can create complete paper dollhouses.

Years ago, when I was teaching junior high math and science, I resorted to paper folding near the end of one school year to illustrate three-dimensional, geometric shapes. My students immediately took to Origami, the art of Japanese paper folding. Within hours, they were creating their own unusual and clever paper creations. One of my students stumbled across a simple fold that lent itself quite nicely to miniature houses and furniture. Although the patterns in most paper-folding books look incomprehensible to the untrained eye, this seventh grade student's basic fold is simple and easy to make. With a bit of practice Origami can become addictive. However, you may want to consult other books on the ancient art.

All you need is Paper!

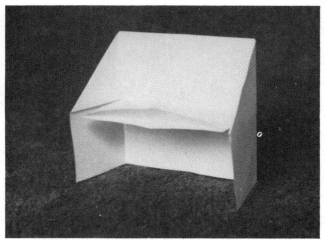

MAKING THE BASIC FOLD (HOUSE)

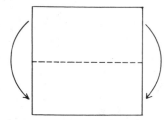

1. Start with square sheet of paper. Fold in half.

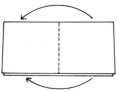

2. Fold in half again to make a center crease line. Open up only this half.

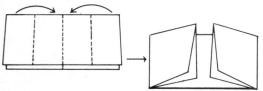

3. Fold each edge to center crease line.

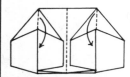 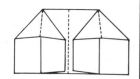

4. Open side flaps partially; push down top corners: sides will flare open.

COUCH

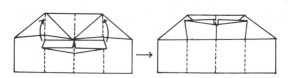

1. Start with Basic Fold; Fold up middle section.

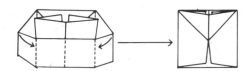

2. Fold outside edges towards center; open up partially; pull middle section down to seat level.

BED

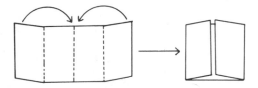

1. Take two ready-made couches and insert into each seat a piece of paper, folded as shown, to form a mattress.

Gingerbread houses are not only fun and easy to make, but great to eat!

TABLE

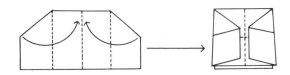

1. *Start with Basic Fold; turn over and fold sides towards middle.*

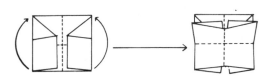

2. *Fold bottom half upwards.*

3. *Turn over and repeat steps 1 & 2. Construct other table half with another sheet of paper. Insert one leaf of table into one leaf of the other table.*

A DOLLHOUSE FOR ALL CELEBRATIONS

An appetizing dollhouse can be made from gingerbread. Cooking up this creation is one project the entire family will want to do together. The finished dollhouse makes a fantastic center piece (and dessert!) at holiday time, especially Thanksgiving and Christmas.

GINGERBREAD DOUGH INGREDIENTS

4 cups whole wheat flour   1 teaspoon allspice
1 cup black-strap molasses 1½ teaspoons ginger
3 eggs   1 teaspoon cinnamon
½ cup butter   ½ teaspoon nutmeg
½ cup raisins

INSTRUCTIONS FOR BAKING AND ASSEMBLING

1. Cut templates out of cardboard for the sides, floor, and roof.

2. Soak ½ cup of raisins in warm water for 2-3 hours. Blend drained raisins in a food mixer until a paste, the consistency of a thick pancake batter, forms. Add water or apple juice as necessary. Use this mixture as your sweetening agent.

3. While the oven preheats to 350° F, mix together the gingerbread ingredients in a large bowl. Blend until thoroughly mixed, then cover the dough, set in the refrigerator until chilled and firm to the touch.

4. Place the chilled dough on a greased cookie sheet and roll it out to ¼" thickness. Using the cardboard templates, cut out the dollhouse patterns in the dough. If you want a shingled roof and log walls, use a knife to draw in these special effects. Now also is a good time to cut out all door and window openings.

5. Bake in the oven for half an hour, or until the dough is firm to your touch. Gingerbread has a way of puffing up and distorting edges and pre-cut windows and doors. While still warm to the touch, trim all openings and edges to the proper dimensions.

6. Allow the trimmed pieces to cool, then add decorations. Peanuts, walnuts and other nuts can form borders on the roof and walls. Dried apple slices can be cut with scissors to make window lattices. Place the apple latticework on the dried apricot windows with glue made of flour and milk. The glue is ready once the milk and flour form a sticky paste. Dried apple slices also make delicious doors.

7. Join walls, floors, and roof parts with the nutritious glue. Add any additional decorations.

8. Bon appetit!

3 Nomadic Playhouses

The spirit of travel and adventure hit me with a vengeance at the age of ten. Beyond afternoon wanderings through a creek that touched our backyard and annual family vacations, my wanderlust was pretty well confined to our immediate neighborhood. One lazy winter afternoon, midway through my fifth-grade year, I discovered *National Geographic Magazine* and it became a special outlet for my travel yearnings in the school library. I read avariciously and spent hours gazing at all the pictures. I traveled to every corner of the globe, tasted every variety of food imaginable, conquered the highest mountains, spoke strange tongues, and slept in magnificent dwellings.

After all the years that have passed one feature article remains crystal clear in my memory, an account of the nomadic Mongolian herdsmen of Central Asia. I can't remember exactly what it was about their life style that fascinated me, but I romanticized life on those Central Asian steppes to the point of dreaming every night about camel trains and game roasting over a smoldering fire.

I mention this early childhood fascination for Central Asia by way of introducing the Mongolian Yurt, one of the most interesting nomadic dwellings ever designed. According to that old edition of *National Geographic* (January 1936, "With the Nomads of Central Asia," by Edward Murray), the actual Mongolian word is "ger," meaning "dwelling". Marco Polo, back in the Thirteenth Century, was one of the first Westerners to come across this remarkable structure. Then and now the fickle temperament of the climate and the availability of good grazing lands dictated the movements of these rugged nomads. The yurt had to be extremely portable to suit their wandering life style. According to Murray, the yurt could be ready for immediate occupancy within ½ hour. And in the same time it took to round up the kids and clean the eating utensils, the entire structure including latticed walls, insulating felt, and canvas covering, could be packed onto a single camel's back.

In recent years, several adventurous groups in this country have been experimenting with the Mongolian yurt as an alternative to traditional dwellings. A few of the hardiest have been living in their nomadic structures for several years and report that they are comfortable, inexpensive to build, and able to weather the coldest winter and the hottest summer.

Recent accounts of these modern-day nomads and my nostalgic recollections of *National Geographic* articles rekindled old fires. And now a parent I thought to myself, "Why not a yurt playhouse, something portable and lightweight, easy to build, and fun to play in?".

I fooled around in our small backyard one weekend trying to find the right combination of materials and angles. Initially, I attempted to build the yurt with the traditional Mongolian latticework walls (similar to the accordion construction of baby-gates). But I soon discovered that the smallest circumference this lattic wall could be curved into created a space much too big for my two-year-old son. This structural problem was finally resolved when I discovered it was much easier to drive the 40" long 1"x2" redwood stakes I bought for the lattice walls directly into the ground. In fact, if there's room in your backyard to sink in a few redwood stakes, building the yurt will be a simple matter.

After you've cut your stakes to size, inscribe a five-foot-diameter circle in the ground where you want the yurt (a five-foot circle will yield an area of nearly twenty-one square feet, much more fitting for the needs of the four-and-under crowd). Drive the stakes into the ground around the perimeter of the circle at 12" intervals. Pound them in at a slight angle so that they slope slightly outward.

The Unique Mongolian Yurt

Pound the yurt's sticks into a circle with radius of five feet.

Place the ends of the roof rafters onto the cable encircling the wall studs. Twist the bicycle rim counter clockwise as you guide the roof into place. This yurt playhouse is designed for preschoolers. Older children will find the quarters cramped.

Now run a ¼" cable or small nylon cord through the eyelets or large staples you have previously fastened one inch down from the top of each stake. Draw the cable tight.

A roof with a skylight is a traditional feature of yurts. Building this aesthetically pleasing roof to traditional plans, however, can be a bit complicated. Fortunately, there's a simple alternative. Drill a ¼" hole 1" to 2" from the end of each of your ten 40" long 1"x2" redwood rafters (the same material used to make the walls). Notch the opposite end of each rafter so that it can rest on the cable strung between the wall supports without slipping off.

Now stitch the roof rafters to the outside of an old 15" bicycle rim (pick up a discard from a local bicycle shop) with thin nylon cord. With all the rafters hanging down from the rim like the limp arms of an octopus, place the notched end of each rafter onto the tension cable between wall studs. You'll need 2-3 sets of extra human arms to get this unwieldy skeleton of boards in place. Once accomplished, twist the wobbly roof at the bicycle rim as far as it will go (twist the rim counter-clockwise). Almost as if by magic, the rafters will settle down securely around the edge of the rim, giving way to an excellent view of the sky above. For a roof that slopes more steeply, and has a bigger skylight, use a larger diameter bicycle rim with the same length rafters.

Close-up of bicycle rim skylight.

Cover the yurt with canvas, leaving an entrance space between two of the redwood stakes. Cut in several windows, and your young nomads can move in. The yurt is surprisingly roomy inside. My son, on several special occasions, has invited my wife and me to visit. Even with the dog wandering in, we were all quite comfortable. But, this yurt is definitely a child's place. The ceiling, (three feet high at the walls and 3½ feet at the center) is not meant for grown-ups.

If you decide to cover the yurt's skeletal frame with canvas, your children can paint their own designs on the cloth before you wrap it around. Potato printing is an especially fun way to individualize the outside of a yurt. Slice one potato in half and, with a paring knife, carefully cut away portions of the exposed tuber, leaving raised designs and patterns of your kids' own making. Coat the carved end of the potato with ink from a pad or with poster paint rolled onto a sheet of newspaper. The young nomads leave their mark by pressing the inked potato onto the canvas (be sure the cloth is resting on a hard, level surface for best results). Don't be surprised if you go through a pound or two of spuds before the project is over. Sheets of thick rubber (you can get them at hobby stores) or wooden blocks make for longer lasting stamps, although, it takes more time and patience to carve in designs.

Chairs and tables have no place in a yurt. Throw an old, discarded rug or piece of carpet over the exposed ground and that's all the kids will need to feel at home. If that old section of carpet isn't enough protection from the damp ground, or if your youngsters prefer to not always sit on the ground, it's an easy matter to fashion a very comfortable and portable stool out of three, fat sticks (or three 1" thick dowels). Cut the three sticks about 2½-3 feet in length. Grab them in a bunch with one hand and loosely tie a rope or heavy cord around the middle with the other hand. Position two of the sticks so that they cross in the middle, forming an "X." Angle the remaining stick leg so that it rests comfortably in the crotch formed by the other two.

The only tricky part is sitting down. The kids will have to slowly lower themselves until they are resting on one of the two branches forming the "X." Be sure the third stick is running directly behind their backs. The stool may give a little as it takes the youngsters' full weight, but will quickly settle down into a stable position. Adjust the sticks as needed for a perfect fit.

If the older kids show an interest in their younger sibling's yurt, they can build their own by increasing the overall dimensions of the circle and slats. For a real yurt clubhouse that can accommodate a gang of kids and can stand up to the

Cover the yurt with canvas and your young nomads can move right in.

heaviest snow falls, take a look at the plans in *Build a Yurt*, by Len Charney (Collier Books, New York, 1974).

TIPIS (Commonly spelled Tepees)

"You have noticed that everything an Indian does is in a circle, and that is because the Power of the World always works in circles, and everything tries to be round. Everything the Power of the World does is done in a circle. The sky is round, and I have heard that the earth is round like a ball, and so are all the stars. The wind in its greatest power, whirls. Birds make their nests in circles, for theirs is the same religion as ours. The sun comes forth and goes down again in a circle. The moon does the same, and both are round. Even the seasons form a great circle in their changing, and always come back again to where they were. The life of a man is a circle from childhood to childhood, and so it is in everything where Power moves. Our tipis were round like the nest of birds, and these were set in a circle . . ."

— Black Elk, Sioux Medicine Man

The word "Tipi" comes from the Sioux language. "Ti" means "to dwell or live" and "pi" means "used for." According to many authorities, the Tipi of the American Plains Indian is the most practical, movable dwelling ever invented. It can be pitched in fifteen minutes by a skilled and experienced individual; it's extremely roomy and well ventilated being cool in summer and warm and dry in winter; it's well lighted; and, it can withstand the severest winds and heaviest downpours.

Indian children often built their own Tipis under their mother's direction. Exact replicas of their parent's nomadic dwellings, these miniature Tipis served as playhouses.

Helping your youngsters build an authentic Indian Tipi playhouse is a fascinating and exciting "history" lesson on our native American culture.

The pattern for your Tipi cover is shown on page 65. You can make it by sewing together 36" wide strips of canvas. Up until the late 1870's, the Plains Indians fashioned their nomadic cones from buffalo hide. But, when the great herds of buffalo began to wane, the Indians turned to canvas. Today there are many types of canvas to choose from. Some of them, such as marine and treated army ducks, are rain proof and mildew resistant, but quite expensive. You might consider buying a less expensive 10 or 12 ounce canvas and treating it yourself with a water repellent such as Thompson's Water Seal. It's recommended that you treat both sides of the canvas (you'll need two to four gallons). If yours is a flame-retardant fabric, it should be treated with Chex-flame (Thompson's Water Seal is incompatible with flame-retardant finishes).

Real Tipis have two layers, the outside cover and an inside dew liner. The liner is approximately four to five feet high and is hung completely around the inside of the Tipi. It seals to the ground. This dew cloth provides excellent insulation and ventilation. It keeps the Tipi dry and comfortable inside. You can make the liner out of the same canvas used for the cover.

INSTRUCTIONS FOR PITCHING A TIPI

1. You'll need thirteen poles, nine in the frame, two for the smoke flaps, one to hoist the canvas into place and one to hold fast the smoke flap cords. Frame and hoisting poles should each be eleven feet long, smoke flap poles nine feet and the smoke flap cord pole four feet. Cedar, lodgepole or Douglas Fir are best. The poles must be straight, no thicker than three inches at the butt and tapering to one inch at the top. Peel the bark and dry each pole before using. If you don't have access to unmilled wood, 2''x4'''s can be cut diagonally from end-to-end and substituted as poles.

2. Lay the three stoutest poles on the Tipi cover. The butts of the two rear poles both go directly to the rear and the butt of the front pole goes to the side (crosswise from the door). All three poles cross at the tie point.

3. Secure the tripod of poles at the tie point with one end of a 35 foot length of rope. Begin with a clove hitch, then finish off the binding with three wrappings and one final clove hitch.

4. Lift up the tripod and walk under the poles, pushing up the bound tops. Once the poles are upright, spread the two back poles so that the three are locked in position.

5. Now put the remaining poles, with the exception of the lifting pole and the two smaller flap poles, in the frame. Position these seven poles so that they are evenly spaced around the tripod.

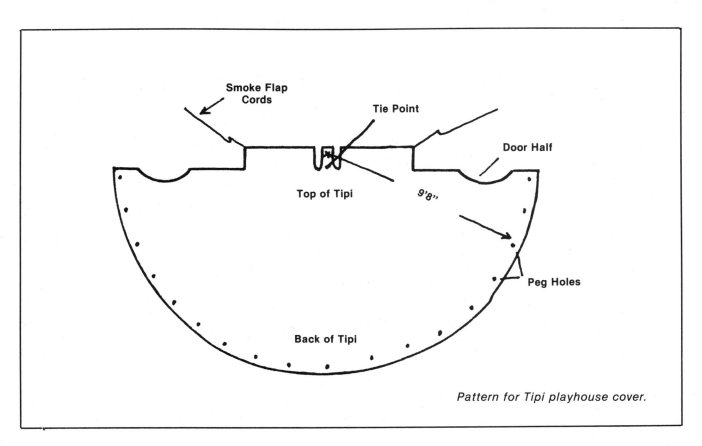

Pattern for Tipi playhouse cover.

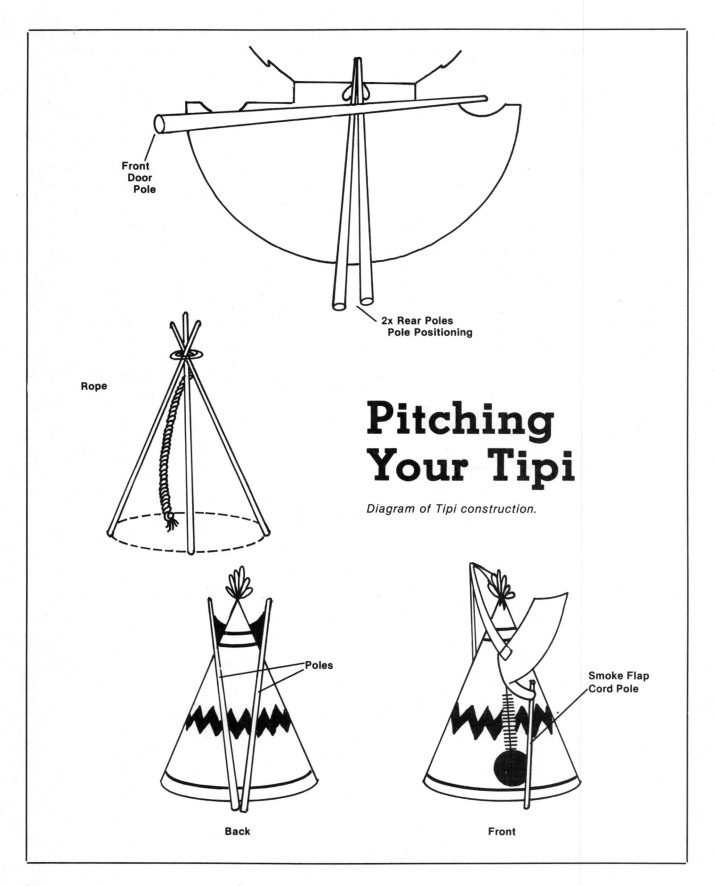

Front
Door
Pole

2x Rear Poles
Pole Positioning

Rope

Pitching Your Tipi

Diagram of Tipi construction.

Poles

Smoke Flap
Cord Pole

Back

Front

6. Tightly wrap the 35 foot length of rope four times around the poles. Anchor the free end of the rope at or near the center point of the Tipi's floor.

7. Next tie two ropes at the tie point of the canvas cover to the top end of the lifting pole. Hoist the entire bundle, pole and folded canvas, by setting the butt of the pole at the Tipi's back (directly opposite the door) and walking it up.

8. Unroll the cover around the poles so that the two canvas sides meet at the front.

9. Lace down the front of the Tipi starting at the top near the smoke flaps.

10. Reposition the poles so that the cover fits snugly, then peg the canvas to the ground.

11. Finally, fasten the smoke flap tie-cords to the two remaining poles.

A first glance at the finished Tipi playhouse may surprise you. The dwelling is not a perfectly symmetrical cone. In fact, a cross section of the Tipi reveals that it's egg shaped! Don't take the Tipi down in hopes of finding your error because you didn't make one. Real Tipis are tilted cones with longer front sides than back sides. And for sound reasons. When the back of the Tipi is placed against prevailing winds, the structure can withstand the fiercest gales. The tilted cone shape also gives you more head room at the back for standing and playing space.

The Plains Indians decorated both the outside and the inside of their Tipis. You and your tribe can do the same, preferably before the canvas is hoisted into place. The kids can sew or paint on their designs. Even crayon drawings can be made and then melted into the fabric with the aid of brown wrapping paper and a hot clothes iron.

Indians use colors, shapes and designs symbolically. For example, among some tribes, circles represent the sun. A red circle symbolizes the morning sun, a yellow circle the setting sun; a triangle represents a Tipi, a zig-zagging line (lightning) signals a storm; bear paws communicate wisdom, magic and medicine. What stories can your kids create on the canvas walls of their Tipis using these symbols and others they create?

For more detailed information on Tipis, *The Indian Tipi: It's History, Construction, and Use,* by Reginald and Gladys Laubien is *must* reading. Diagrams, sketches and original photographs will bring this unique, native American dwelling closer to home. And if you're interested in setting up an authentic Tipi for the older, larger kids in your household or just want more design ideas, write to the following Tipi manufacturers for their catalogs (be sure to enclose a self-addressed, stamped envelope for a quick reply):

Goodwin-Cole Tentmakers
1315 Alhambra Blvd.
Sacramento, CA 95816

Jeb and Caroline
Nomadics Tipi Makers
17671 Snow Creek Rd.
Bend, OR 97701

Morning Star
Box 11000
Aspen, CO 81611

Tipi Workshop
8404 Oyster Bay Road NW
Olympia, WA 98502

BALANCING AND CLIMBING

Tipis inspire pow-wow's and social play — a scouting party venturing off into the dense forest and underbrush in search of wild game. They will encounter fallen logs and rough boulders to scramble over, a feat requiring balance and large muscle coordination. If logs and boulders are not a part of your backyard, it's simple to provide equipment that lets your children practice balancing and climbing skills. Balance beams simply can be 4 x 4's on the ground or block supports cut to hold a 2 x 4 beam either horizontally or vertically. Or you can build the balance beam and support box designed by the Stanley Tool Works.

MATERIALS

2 pieces	4'x8'x¾'' exterior fir plywood for high support box
1 piece	4'x8'x¾'' exterior fir plywood for low support box
6 pieces	2''x4''x10'' select structural fir for balance rails
1 pound	8d galvanized common nails
3	⅜'' x4'' carriage bolts (be sure to add washers under nuts)
3	5⁄16''x7'' carriage bolts (be sure to add washers under nuts)

Support Boxes for Balance Beam

(Courtesy The Stanley Works, Inc.)

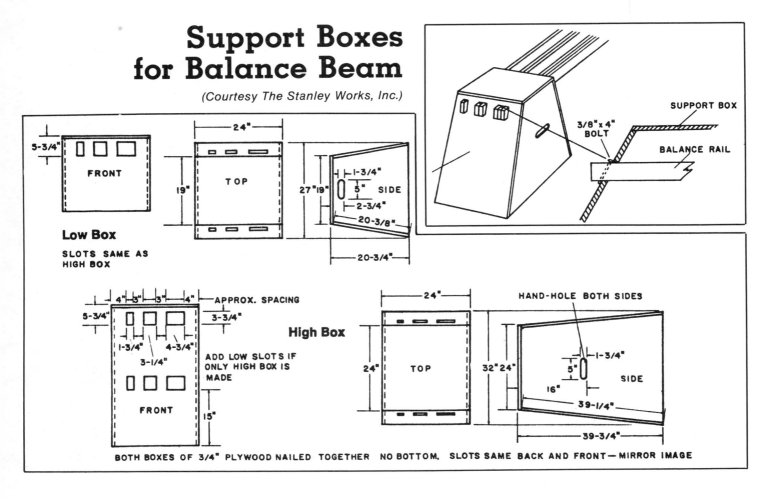

INSTRUCTIONS FOR BUILDING SUPPORT BOXES AND BEAMS

Support boxes are made with butt joints. Since the front and back pieces meet the top piece at an angle, use a surform tool on the tops of the front and back pieces to chamfer the edges so the edges meet the top pieces squarely. Set 8d nails about every 6 inches.

To make sure the slots for balance rails in the front and rear panel line up, clamp these two panels together and make slots in both pieces at the same time. Dress slots with a surform file so rails will slip in and out easily when you wish to change arrangement. When rails are in use, be sure they are secured with bolts as indicated.

The 2"x4"s that make up double and triple balance beams should be fastened together with 8d nails. Age and physical ability of children determine how wide the balance beams should be. You may not want to make three rails. If you make more than one rail, be certain that only one balance beam is used at a time.

A ramp also helps develop a child's eye-foot coordination. A ramp can be a ladder leaning at an angle against a wall, a solid fence or another play structure. A balance beam, one end higher than the other, makes a good ramp. For an additional challenge, vary the shape of the ramp making it wide at one end and narrowing it down to a point at the other. Or you can substitute a round beam for a rectangular ramp (telephone pole-sized logs to tightrope thin cables).

Climbing is another skill which, once mastered, provides children with a sense of confidence in their physical prowess. Upon seeing a tree, the first thought that enters the minds of many children is, "What's the best way to get to the top?". Of course, kids will look to other obstacles besides trees to test their abilities, as many a fretful parent has learned upon entering the living room to find their offspring perched precariously on top a wobbly pile of chairs and tables. Even homes with limited play space can provide children with safer climbing structures. Build your kids a ladder house out of cardboard and 1" dowels.

Ladder House

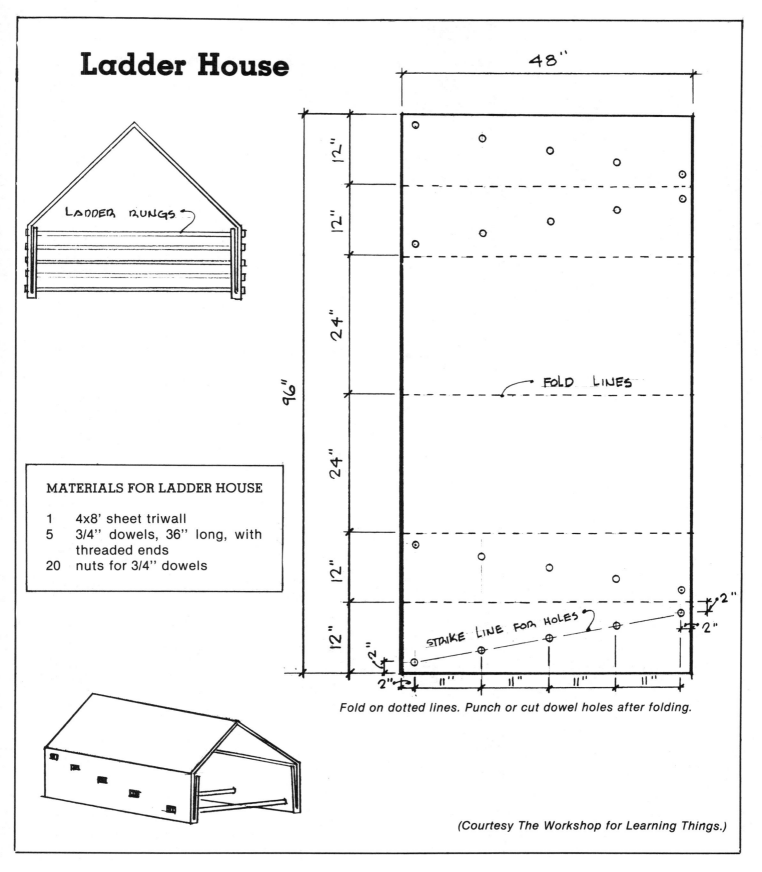

MATERIALS FOR LADDER HOUSE

1	4x8' sheet triwall
5	3/4" dowels, 36" long, with threaded ends
20	nuts for 3/4" dowels

LADDER RUNGS

48"

96"

12"
12"
24"
24"
12"
12"

FOLD LINES

STRIKE LINE FOR HOLES

2"
2"
2"

2"   2"   11"   11"   11"   11"

Fold on dotted lines. Punch or cut dowel holes after folding.

(Courtesy The Workshop for Learning Things.)

Balance beams help children develop eye-foot coordination and promote large muscle development.

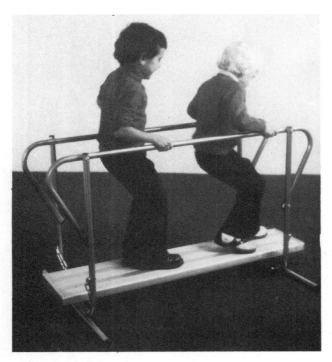

This sway-bridge challenges the coordination of both handicapped and non-handicapped children. The unit can accommodate up to five kids in leg and torso exercise to improve balance and coordination. (Courtesy Constructive Playthings Co.)

THE STEGEL

A single structure that allows your braves to climb, balance, crawl and jump is the Stegel (rhymes with bagel). The Stegel is a multi-purpose balance beam and climbing structure that includes two large sawhorses, three long balance beams, two ladders, a slide, and various props. That adds up to a variety of activities for your children. The Stegel provides narrow spaces to crawl through, beams to balance on, ladders to climb up and down and much more.

But the Stegel is more than just a piece of exercise equipment. The Stegel challenges children to know and define their bodily limits. It forces them to coordinate their movements in order to climb and balance their way over, under and through the maze of boards. These activities lay the foundation for such spatial concepts as "next to", "behind", "under", and "in front of". As a prop for dramatic play, the Stegel can extend group interaction or make a story come to life. With a little imagination, kids can change the Stegel into a tightrope in a circus or the Troll's bridge from "The Three Billy Goats Gruff".

This ingenious piece of equipment was designed for elementary P.E. programs, but with certain modifications (wider balance beams and more gently sloping balance beam walks), the Stegel can be used with preschool children aged three to five years. The Stegel also has been used successfully with handicapped children, especially neurologically impaired and emotionally disturbed kids. If you do plan to use the apparatus with these children, first consult a licensed therapist for instructions in safe and proper usage.

Correctly used, the Stegel can lead both the handicapped and the non-handicapped child through challenging and satisfying physical activities. As children progress to more and more complicated feats of balancing and climbing, they gain the self-confidence needed to tackle new and more challenging situations. Self-confidence and a good self-image are important for the emotional well-being of all children.

Additional information on the Stegel and its use is available in *Stegel Movement Activities* (1978). Although written for classroom use (preschool through university), the book is easily adaptable for home use. It can be purchased for $3.95, from Front Row Experience, Suite 217, 564 Central Avenue, Alameda, CA 94501.

"The Stegel"

Many different props can be used with the
Stegel including slides and ladders, for example.
The Stegel is a perfect apparatus for action-
packed dramatic play.

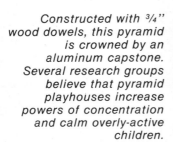

*Constructed with ¾"
wood dowels, this pyramid
is crowned by an
aluminum capstone.
Several research groups
believe that pyramid
playhouses increase
powers of concentration
and calm overly-active
children.*

GREAT PYRAMID PLAYHOUSES

In recent years, archeologists and scientists have written much about the Great Pyramid in Giza, Egypt. Built close to 4000 years ago, the pyramid today remains one of the most precisely and accurately constructed structures of all time. Precision aside, a number of additional features of the pyramid mystify and puzzle modern-day investigators. For example, animals that have wandered in, lost their way and died, have been discovered perfectly preserved in a mummified state. This phenomenon and others have caused many scientists and laypeople alike to question the "secret powers" of the Great Pyramid.

Recently, several independent researchers have reported duplicating the same strange happenings in scale models of the Great Pyramid fashioned from many different materials. Foods remain fresh longer; coffee tastes less bitter and tobacco milder; people are able to concentrate better; razor blades stay sharp longer; the claims made are numerous. Some reports have been verified by intense research, while some remain highly speculative.

One research group has conducted tests with children and pyramids. This group reports that a pyramid playhouse increases comprehension and instigates a calming effect on children who play inside. Considerably more intensive research remains to be done before any of these claims can be substantiated.

In the meantime, why not build your own portable pyramid playhouse? The playhouse can be made of any material, just be sure the edge length of the pyramid's four faces is 4.9% less than the edge length of the base, while the overall vertical height is 36.4% less than the base edge length . For example, a pyramid with a base of 72" will have sides of 68.5" and an overall height of 45.8".

Once assembled, you can cover the pyramid with any material you wish, or leave it open. Several "pyramidologists" report that the pyramid's *powers* are enhanced when the structure is crowned with a pyramidal capstone made of copper or aluminum. In order to work properly, all investigators say the structure must be aligned with one pair of sides running exactly North-South.

The following phenomena have been observed with pyramids. Can you and your children prove or disprove these with your own homemade pyramid?

- alfalfa sprouts grown in the pyramid or sprouted in water kept under the pyramid overnight last longer after harvesting than sprouts grown outside the pyramid
- bitter and sour foods kept in the pyramid for several hours become milder
- sweet fruits become sweeter
- cut flowers take longer to die if placed in pyramid-treated water
- pickled foods become mellower in taste
- frozen foods defrosted under a pyramid have a richer, more natural flavor

- fresh fruit and vegetables treated under the pyramid an hour before storage in the refrigerator or fruit bowl will last about twice as long as normal
- bread without preservatives stays fresh in the original wrapper for up to seven weeks.

CARDBOARD TABLE AND CHAIR

If you've read this far in the chapter, all you and your kids have to sit on while conducting your experiments is a three-stick stool. Comfortable, but perhaps not to everyone's liking. With a sharp mat knife and a metal straight edge, your children can design and build their own inexpensive, "kid-size" furniture in a relatively short period of time. All they need in the way of building materials are sections of double or triple wall cardboard. Hardware stores and appliance dealers are good sources of cardboard. Offer to do these business people a favor by hauling off the cardboard clutter yourself.

Building with cardboard is a tremendous amount of fun. Mistakes don't have serious consequences, the material is easy to work with, and the results — from sketched design to finished product — are immediate. Making cardboard furniture is a great family project, either after weekday dinners or on lazy weekends.

Single wall cardboard consists of a fluted middle layer sandwiched in between two smooth surfaces. Double wall cardboard has two layers and triple wall, or tri-wall, has three layers. Tri-wall is the strongest — nearly as strong as wood — and is best for constructing furniture. Tri-wall also is most difficult to obtain. If you're unable to locate this versatile building material, make your own by laminating together single and double wall sheets with carpenter's white glue or panel adhesive.

When cardboard is used in a horizontal position (table tops, chair seats), the flutes should run in the direction of the longest dimension for greatest strength. In a vertical position, such as the side of a chair or legs of a table, be sure the flutes run up and down, not sideways.

Tools you'll find useful in cardboard carpentry include a sabre saw equipped with a knife blade, a yard-stick, utility knife, 6" spring clamps, a fine-toothed hand saw and a key-hole saw.

With this working knowledge of cardboard and the proper tools at hand, the kids can construct this sturdy table and stool for their playhouses.

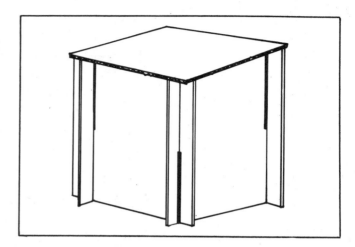

TABLE & CHAIR PLANS

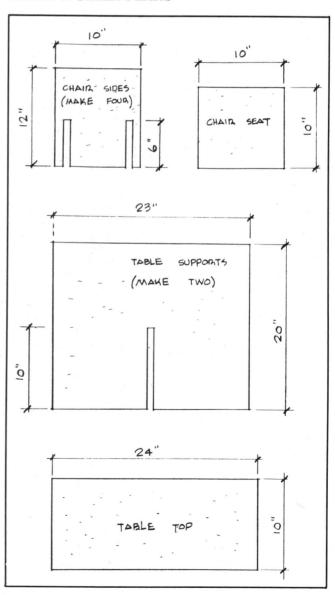

The Cardboard Camper

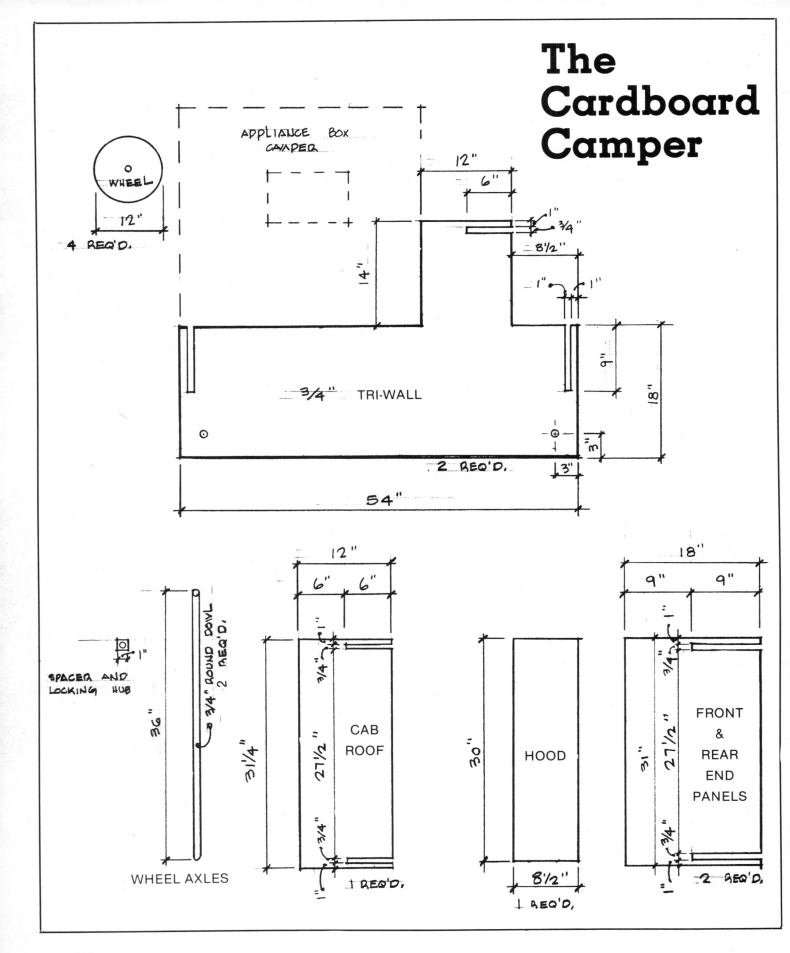

WHEEL
12"
4 REQ'D.

APPLIANCE BOX CAMPER

12"
6"
1"
3/4"
8½"
1"
1"
14"

3/4" TRI-WALL

9"
18"
3"
3"

2 REQ'D.

54"

SPACER AND LOCKING HUB
1"
36"
3/4" ROUND DOWL
2 REQ'D.
WHEEL AXLES

12"
6"
6"
1"
3/4"
31¼"
27½"
3/4"
CAB ROOF
1 REQ'D.

30"
HOOD
8½"
1 REQ'D.

18"
9"
9"
1"
3/4"
31"
27½"
FRONT & REAR END PANELS
3/4"
1"
2 REQ'D.

The pick-up body is constructed from double wall cardboard. The camper shell is a washing machine packing carton. The wheels are made from two pieces of tri-wall glued together and are held in place by 1" wood dowel axles. Small, wood spacers prevent the wheels from rubbing against the pick-up body. The wheels are kept on the axles with "locking hubs", wood blocks drilled to slip over the axles and fastened down with wood screws. Painting the camper creates as much excitement as driving it!

Telephone poles lift this backyard platform high off the ground. Smaller logs create the platform's deck.

This fort, a maze of interconnecting tunnels and secret chambers, has been built primarily with railroad ties.

With practical cardboard experience under their belts, your children are now ready to tackle a playhouse modeled after a truly modern, nomadic vehicle — a pick-up truck with camper. This playhouse, highly representative of our nomadic way of life, is one in which the kids won't have to be backseat drivers. Don't be surprised, though, if the younger kids turn the camper into a fire engine (a few 3' pieces of garden hose attached to the sides will synch the conversion) or a manned space probe to Mars (five-gallon drums, the kind ice cream is packed in, make excellent helmets).

This design is popular with children ages 2-9. But remember, it's just a basic design. Let your children add any special features they want or completely change it when the mood strikes them.

RECYCLING NOMADIC MATERIALS

More and more school yards and playgrounds are beginning to look like the recycling centers for the artifacts of our nomadic way of life. Tires are transformed into climbing structures and swings and even discarded vehicles themselves are being converted into jungle gyms and club houses. In this era of conservation and recycling, it makes a lot of sense. You can use these same reusable materials on a smaller scale to create playhouses and exercise equipment in your own backyard.

Tires can be lined up for walking on and jumping through, climbing inside and resting, or, when no one's around, you can use them as nomadic clothes lines.

BUILDING WITH TIRES

We fail to notice when discarding our old tires that there is still a lot of life left in them. With a little imagination, used tires (get them from trucking and heavy construction contractors, tire dealers, recapping outfits or wrecking yards) can be recycled into wonderful swings, climbing structures, playhouses, tunnels and see-saws.

First, a few words on the mechanics of tire building. There are three ways to join tires: tread to tread; sidewall to sidewall; and tread to sidewall. To fasten together two or more tires, punch or drill a $\frac{7}{16}$" hole through the adjacent surfaces, then slip a $\frac{3}{8}$" cap screw carrying a $\frac{3}{8}$" fender washer and a $\frac{3}{4}$" steel washer through the hole. Secure this unit with a second $\frac{3}{8}$" fender washer synched down with a $\frac{3}{8}$" bolt. To prevent loosening, add a lock washer and second nut. Use a one inch auger bit to drill drainage holes in the finished tire project.

A very simple playhouse can be made from bus or truck tires. Set two parallel tires upright and approximately three feet apart. Place a third and a fourth tire at either end and bolt them to each of the first two tires. Leave the openings in the structure's four sides, or cover them with blankets. If you have a large enough sandy area, tire playhouses need not be bolted together, but temporarily sunk in the sand. When you construct temporary tire spaces, be sure they are stable and cannot collapse on small children playing inside.

Passenger car tires bolted sidewall-to-sidewall make inviting crawl-through spaces. Be sure to lay out the tunnels so that you have both visual and physical access to all portions, especially important for parents of preschoolers. Giant tractor tires, either upright or flat on the ground, make

Tire See-Saw

◄*Half an old tractor or truck tire easily converts into a high-rocking seesaw. (Designers John Harding and Associates. Courtesy A Playground for All Children, New York Department of City Planning.)*

This tire swing can hold three youngsters at a time. Note large eyebolts spaced equidistant around the tire's perimeter. It can spin and swing, using a swivel hub allows a guardian to "wind up" the unit and relax as the swing unwinds. Note low barrier which cautions anyone from walking into the path of the swing. (Courtesy A Playground for All Children. New York Department of City Planning.)

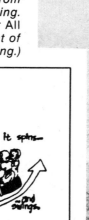

cozy spaces to curl up in and let the world go by. Stack the monsters on top of each other, and they become a hollow mountain retreat. One enterprizing nursery school in Los Angeles, California, made a climbing wall of used motorcycle tires by tying them tread-to-tread with pieces of sturdy rope. Not only did this "donut" wall serve as an ideal partition between play areas, but it quickly became a popular climbing structure.

Earlier, I described how to make a swing suitable for one child. Swings, however, need not be limited to one person. With a large bus or tractor tire, swinging can become a social activity. Drill three holes equi-distant from each other on the same side of the tire about two inches from the tread. Secure three support chains, ropes, or cables to the tire through these holes. Fasten the supports to a swivel three feet from the tire (the swivel guards against pinched fingers by preventing the three supports from twisting). Attach the swing via one sturdy cable to an overhang or to a thick tree branch. Be sure to wrap a section of tire around the tree branch to protect it against cable wear and tear.

Young children love to spin round and round on revolving tire swings. Most adults, however, can take only a little twirling before anxiously seeking out solid, immovable ground. There's a reason for this seeming lack of "adventure" among adults. Grown-ups have a well-developed sense of balance. Our vestibular mechanism or balance center (located in the inner ear) no longer needs a great deal of swinging input to teach our bodies how to function in space. The sense of balance in young kids, on the other hand, isn't as well developed. The more stimulating the input channeled through their vestibular mechanism, the better able they are to learn how to coordinate the movements of their bodies through space.

Provide your kids with a safe and stimulating swinging environment by keeping in mind the load the swing will be handling. If you're planning to use rope, ¾" rope is a hefty size (½" or ⅝" polyethylene or nylon works well, too). Though more expensive, cable is quite a bit more durable than rope. One-quarter inch cable will serve most needs. The most durable and expensive is chain (¼" or ⁵⁄₁₆"). The following figures will give you an idea of the safe load limits for each of these supporting materials.

¾" hemp rope	1000 lbs.
¼" cable	1700 lbs.
³⁄₁₆" cable	1200 lbs.
¼" chain	2500 lbs.
⁵⁄₁₆" chain	5000 lbs.

In some cases, you may have to sink posts as supports for the swings (where there are no suitable overhangs or trees in your yard). If you do sink posts, bury them anywhere from 2' to 6' underground, depending on the average load the posts will be carrying.

Additional safety factors to take into account when building a swing are: 1. The immediate area

Cable spools are integral parts of this backyard play unit. A single, giant spool forms the platform in the background while smaller spools help girder the bridge and slide.

around swings should be clear to avoid any interference with the moving swing; 2. The bottom of the swing should be no more than three feet off the ground; 3. Wrap exposed cable ends with a protective covering such as cloth tape.

You can stretch the life of tires a long way; the same is true for inner tubes. We generally think of them as inexpensive life rafts for swimming. But these inflatable rubber donuts also make excellent play objects for use on solid ground. Bouncing on them, rolling over them, or using them as a dynamic circular group bench are a few of the possibilities. Why not lash three to four together with surgical tubing and create an elastic "barrel" to roll around in? Your kids will come up with many more ideas. Just be sure that the tube's valve stem is padded or deflected in some way so that it doesn't harm anyone.

MORE BUILDABLE EXPENDABLES

Cable spools are those large wooden cylinders ropes and wire are stored on. Occasionally contractors will discard the spools at their building sites, leaving them for the clean-up crew to dispose of. Sometimes older, faultier spools can be obtained directly from the utility company. Industrial hardware dealers also may have several discards ready for pick-up.

When left standing upright, spools are natural climbing structures. With several units of different sizes, you can create an environment that really challenges the physical coordination of children three to ten years old. Or carefully remove several of the middle slats and you've got yourself an entrance to a cozy, cylinder house. The bigger the spool, the bigger the house.

Once the kids have moved into their spool playhouse, they'll need something in which to store their treasures. A functional storage chest consists of nothing more than a large upright box. Inside are stacked shoeboxes that have the outward-facing ends cutoff for easy access. Or you can nail together peach or pear crates to create a storage space for valuable odds-'n-ends.

An entire cable spool can be made into a storage space in-the-round with an upper play deck (see photo page 79). Cut six 2x4's so that each of their lengths equals that of the upright spool, with enough left over to form the supports for a guard rail. Fasten each of these 2x4's with lag screws to the spool. Now cut five more 2x4's to size and fasten them to the tops of the wooden uprights. These five form the deck's protective railing. Add a "fence" to keep the kids safely contained on the upper level. In the structure pictured on this page, the "fence" is a section of rope stretched in the shape of a giant "W" between the uprights. Add an entrance ladder to the section without the guardrail or "fence".

Cut out ten shelf sections (enough for two rows) from ½" particle board or plywood. Place each shelf between uprights and nail in place. Don't put shelving under the entrance ladder.

An old rug cut to shape and several soft pillows make this an ideal indoor storage/play unit for any preschooler. The shelves are "kid-height" and perfect for storing valuable treasures.

For more recycling possibilities, hunt up some metal drums. Leave them on the ground for crawl-through tunnels; raise them up on saw horses for heightened climbing and crawling challenges; combine them with a slide or ladder; or elevate one end of the drum and use it as a tunnel-slide. Drums with sharp lips can be taken to drum companies and the edges rolled for safety.

Wooden drums (barrels), too, can be transformed into play equipment. Build a "treadmill" by running a pipe axle through the center of a barrel's

With several slats removed, a discarded cable spool transforms into a cylinder playhouse.

"Fun Treasures for Free"

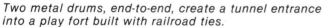

With the addition of a ladder, shelves and protective ▶ railing, this cable spool becomes an attractive and functional platform and storage unit.

Two metal drums, end-to-end, create a tunnel entrance into a play fort built with railroad ties.

Metal drums and a floating platform with flexible sealing strip to contain the water below make a "balance walk" for both handicapped and non-handicapped kids. (Designed by Nicholas Quennel Associates. Courtesy A Playground for All Children, New York Department of City Planning.)

With coats of paint, old sailboats and motorboats can be reconditioned into outdoor play spaces.

long dimension. Suspend the whole unit — barrel and axle — above the ground between two upright posts. Leave enough space between the barrel and the ground so that the wooden drum spins freely. Hang a bar directly over this unique treadmill, and the kids, holding on for support, can run miles without ever leaving the yard.

For a smooth rolling, high rocking see-saw, attach a ten foot 2"x12" plank to the barrel with ⅜" long screws (you may have to brace the plank to the barrel with small wooden blocks). Let the kids sit at either end of the plank and have them push off lightly with their legs. The barrel-fulcrum will do the rest.

Don't forget about discarded automobiles and boats! Once all sharp corners and protrusions have been removed, these castoffs are ready-made playhouses. Certainly being remodeled into a playhouse is a much more honorable fate then being left to rust in a junkyard or tossed about endlessly in the surf. When space and materials are available, refurbishing an old row boat or car can be an exciting project.

LEARNING PLAY UNIT

Telephone poles and concrete sewer pipe are main components in this tunnel-slide structure. The apparatus was designed and built by PEECH (Precise Early Education of Children with Handicaps). The tunnel-slide play area is just one piece of equipment used in the PEECH program at the University of Illinois, in Urbana-Champaign, for the education of multiply handicapped children, ages three to five.

"The nature of the caregiver-child interaction is an important aspect of a program for preschool handicapped children," explains the Director of the program, Dr. Merle Karnes. "Children will function more effectively in an environment that has established consistent expectations and limits from day-to-day. Many preschool, handicapped children have not yet acquired the skills necessary to make decisions, solve problems, and to interact in a meaningful and growing way with the environment. Consequently, in a *structured* approach, the caregiver plans activities for the children based on their needs and assists and reinforces them during the activity."

One of the principles of the PEECH program is language development. "The development of language skills provides a foundation for all areas of cognition", Dr. Karnes emphasizes. "To be successful in school and in life, a person must be proficient in language processing skills. Acquiring new concepts and ideas, relating those concepts and ideas in new ways and communicating them to others, are skills that are essential for an individual to fully develop his potential. It cannot be over-emphasized that acquisition of language skills is highly related to almost all facets of school success. Since language development is cumulative, attention to helping children develop language processing skills should begin at an early age."

The tunnel-slide structure can provide many opportunities for developing these all-important language skills. In labeling children's activities and in giving one-and-two-step directions ("Crawl through the pipe. Now climb up the ladder, walk to the pole and slide down"), receptive language is improved. In discussing incidents or procedures, parents can help young children expand their expressive powers ("My, you went through the tunnel quickly. How did you go so fast? What's the best way for you go get up on the platform now?").

To fully utilize structures such as PEECH's tunnel-slide area for the positive, cognitive, and emotional growth of handicapped children, consult a licensed teacher or occupational therapist.

The "PEECH" Playground

(Courtesy PEECH project.)

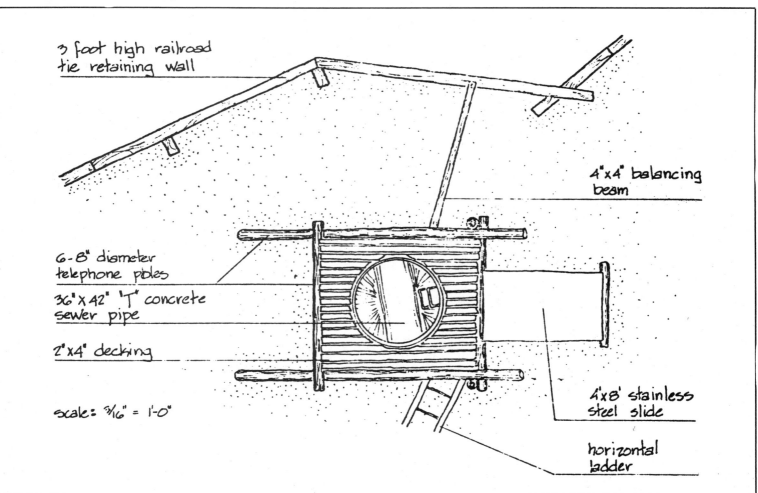

3 foot high railroad tie retaining wall

4"x4" balancing beam

6-8" diameter telephone poles

36"x 42" 'T' concrete sewer pipe

2"x4" decking

scale: 3/16" = 1'-0"

4'x8' stainless steel slide

horizontal ladder

Cardboard Dwellings

Perhaps a child invented the first "cardboard dwelling". One thing for certain, it has to be the least expensive playhouse — and yet provokes a lot of creativity.

4
Modular and Dome Playhouses

If you think construction costs are high these days, why not be the first on your block to build a paper house — a paper playhouse, that is. Actually, full-scale paper houses aren't new. Back in 1853, an enterprising group built a complex of ten paper cottages plus a ten-room villa in Australia. During World War II, the U.S. War Production Board asked the Institute of Paper Chemistry to develop a portable house — made of paper, of course — that could be mass-produced and used for the homeless in disaster areas. The Institute designed a house made of inch-thick chipboard, fabricated from wastepaper, strengthened by sulfur so it could be easily sawed and nailed, and coated with fire-proof paint. The house weighed 1029 pounds and the designers figured it would last at least a year. Thirty-five years later, the house was still standing!

You and the kids can design and build your own paper house with a minimum of trouble. The structure won't weigh 1029 pounds nor will it last thirty-five years. But, it will provide hours of fun for the six-and-under crowd. First, get your hands on a large cardboard box in which an appliance (refrigerator, stove, washer or dryer) was shipped. Decide where you want the door and windows, then cut them out with a sharp utility knife. If the door is to swing open and shut, cut only on three sides, and score and bend the attached side to serve as the hinge. With a few extra pieces of cardboard and some strips of masking or duct tape, add a gable roof. The young members of your family will have great fun outdoors on a sunny day or just as much fun indoors on a cold, blustery winter day.

Box houses can be contagious. Once you've built one, it's easy to build another, then another, and yet another. When the kids have three or more, push the cardboard dwellings together, cut in connecting doors, then give the children paint and

brushes and let them paint their new city. If cities aren't your family's style, line up the large containers end-to-end and cut passageways in each adjoining crate to form a tunnel maze.

Even damaged cardboard containers can be put to good use. Cut rectangular, square and triangular panels from the salvaged cartons and punch holes along the edges with a big paper punch, a knitting needle or a nail set. Cut out doors and windows, punch the needed holes, then stitch appropriate panels together with twine or plastic clothesline. The more panels and space available, the larger and more complex your kids can make their structure. Depending on whether they're creating inside or outside, children can decorate their playhouse or maze with poster paints, crayons or cut-and-glue-on pictures from magazines and newspapers.

One alternative to the "stitch-it" method is to build with notched pieces of cardboard. These cardboard panels are held together simply by interlocking the notches of two separate units. Cut each notch a bit longer than half the vertical height of each panel and in a width that will just accommodate the thickness of the cardboard you're using. Vary the number and angles of notches in each cardboard panel, thus setting the stage for a variety of structures. A little building practice with the panels will soon give you a thorough knowledge of what works best for your kids, and your kids will have the basic logic behind constructing a cardboard shelter.

Once you've got the right combination of panels stand back and let the master builders get to work. Houses will be torn down just as quickly as they go up. Kids jump from idea to finished product in the blink of an eye. The joy for them is the pleasure of doing. Rarely will children spend a great deal of time sitting back and admiring their completed handiwork.

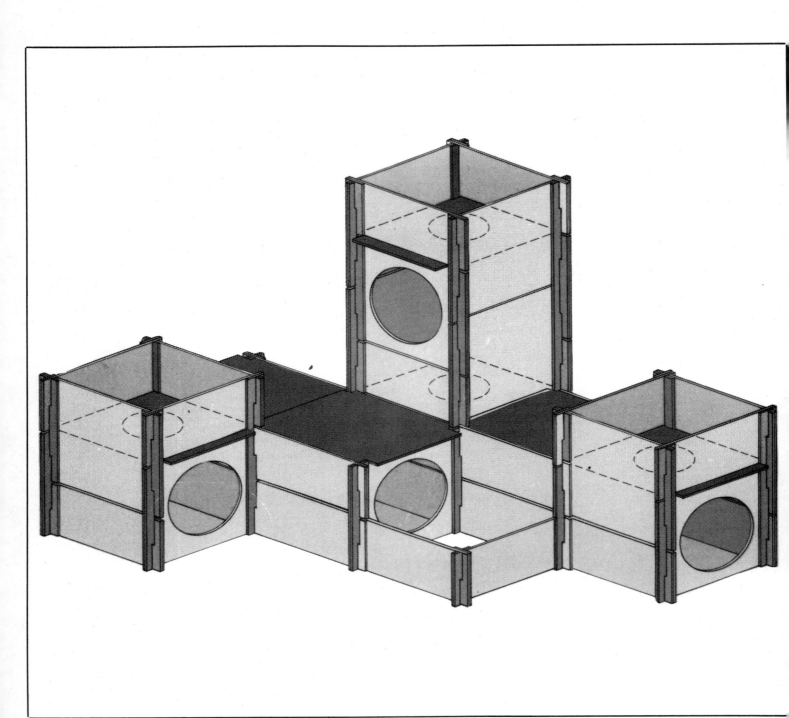

(Courtesy of Gregg Fleishman and Dan Hanrahan)

Modular Building
with the
Play Panel Structure

PLAY PANEL STRUCTURE

Play Panel Structure is a modular system of panels that fit together to form cubular spaces in an infinite variety of combinations.

Gregg Fleishman developed the system for use at Modern Playschool — Play Mountain Place, Los Angeles. It replaces boxes and planks as a means to construct clubhouses, forts, castles, bridges, etc. Connectors such as bolts, screws or other pieces aren't required. Gravity holds the elements down; interlocking slots hold them together. It is a play environment that can be changed daily by kids, enhancing their creativity and increasing their confidence in their abilities to positively affect their environment. Once the panels have been completed, children become the creators of their own play structure.

The system consists of panels comprised of five different shapes. Combinations of these shapes provide the elements necessary to create structures.

For the four foot module panels, three 4' x 8' sheets of ½" thick plywood make the elements of one cube. In larger structures, the ratio of fillers to walls becomes lower, although not significantly if the structure's shape becomes complex. For one cube, make eight half fillers, four full fillers, four half wall panels, two full wall panels, and one floor panel. For more cubes, just multiply these quantities by the number of cubes desired. See page 86 for patterns and dimensions of each panel.

Note that with larger structures, the number of cubular spaces created can become greater than the number of possible individual cubes due to the fact that spaces in between cubes become cubes themselves.

Because the panels are made of plywood, you can cut them to their proper shape with common hand tools. Edges can easily be sanded or routed to ease all sharp corners. Paint or varnish surfaces and edges to resist abrasion and weathering that will occur during use. For exterior use, the plywood and coating should be of the best quality possible. The greater the care in preparation, the longer the panels will last and the least they will cost in the end.

The dimensions shown are for use with ½" thick plywood. The resultant panels are of a size that can be used by all children and adults. If you wish panels specifically or only for use with smaller children (6 or under), use ⅜" thick plywood and scale down the panel dimensions accordingly.

Help your kids assemble the structures on a flat surface starting from the bottom and working up. Some planning must go into the organization of this play environment so that assembly can proceed in an orderly manner. As pieces stack on top of one another, all of those above an incorrectly located piece must be removed in order to relocate or remove it.

Begin assembly by holding in position the two lower half wall panels and half fillers as shown on page 87. For the structure to extend horizontally in either direction in the plane of the panel surfaces, replace the half filler pieces with half panel pieces to the side to which you wish the structure to extend. The continuation of the structure can go on until you wish it to stop.

Continue with the assembly by placing, from above, the full wall panels and full fillers shown in blue. This secures in position the half panels below and awaits the placement of the half panels from above. If you want the structure to extend along the plane of the full wall panels, just replace the fillers on the side to which you wish to extend it with full wall panels.

The Basic Cube Structure

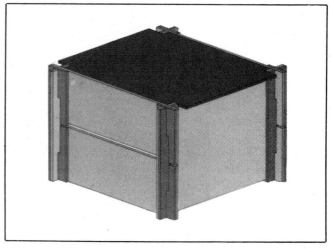

(Courtesy of Gregg Fleishman and Dan Hanrahan)

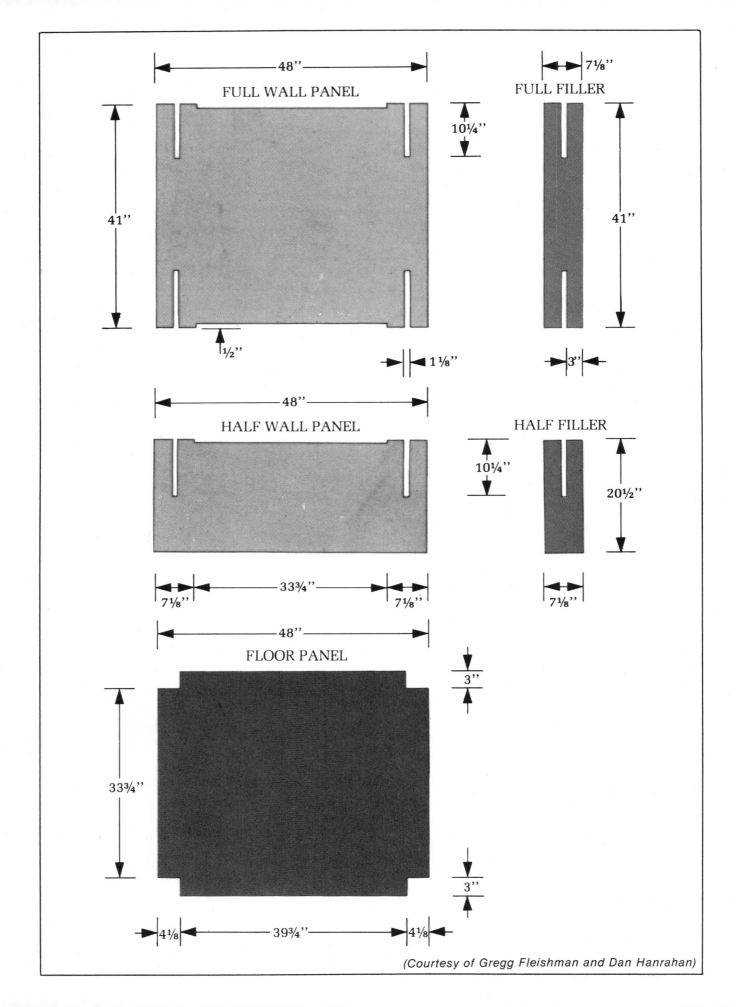

FULL WALL PANEL

48"

41"

10¼"

½"

1⅛"

FULL FILLER

7⅛"

41"

3"

HALF WALL PANEL

48"

10¼"

33¾"

7⅛"

7⅛"

HALF FILLER

20½"

7⅛"

FLOOR PANEL

48"

3"

33¾"

3"

4⅛"

39¾"

4⅛"

(Courtesy of Gregg Fleishman and Dan Hanrahan)

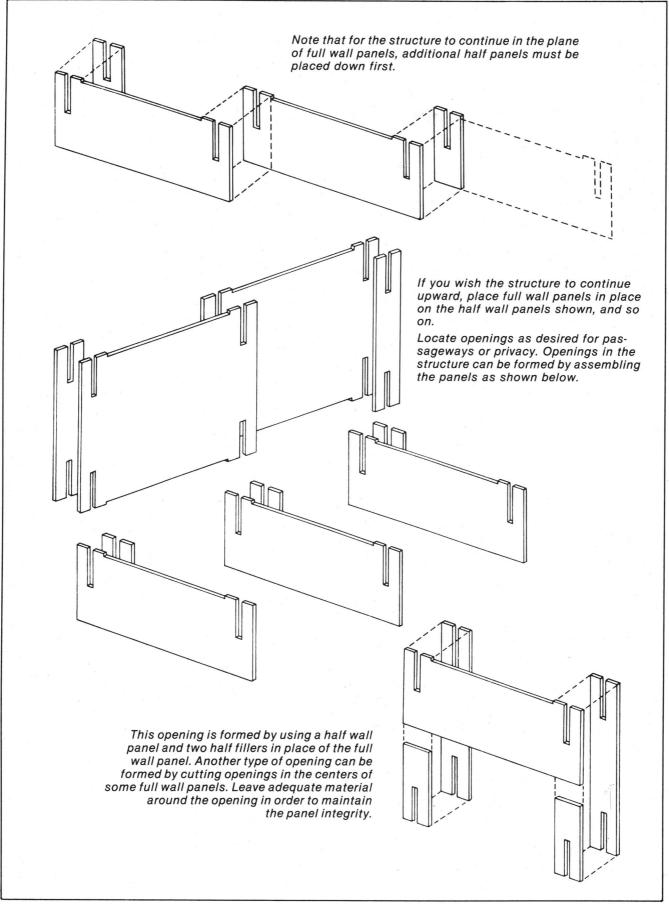

Note that for the structure to continue in the plane of full wall panels, additional half panels must be placed down first.

If you wish the structure to continue upward, place full wall panels in place on the half wall panels shown, and so on.

Locate openings as desired for passageways or privacy. Openings in the structure can be formed by assembling the panels as shown below.

This opening is formed by using a half wall panel and two half fillers in place of the full wall panel. Another type of opening can be formed by cutting openings in the centers of some full wall panels. Leave adequate material around the opening in order to maintain the panel integrity.

(Courtesy of Gregg Fleishman and Dan Hanrahan)

The Sky's The Limit

*Basic
assembly
of the
structure.*

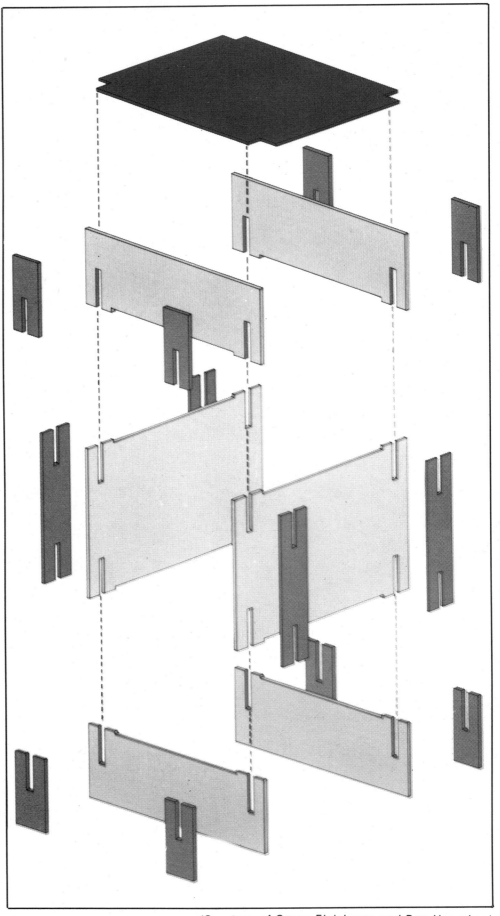

(Courtesy of Gregg Fleishman and Dan Hanrahan)

Build a Mongolian yurt and let your children dream of far-off lands. All it takes is an afternoon and your imagination.

Even a pyramid of ¾" dowels can create a "space" for play. Covering for the structure is optional. As you can see here, defined play space need not always be enclosed.

Any way you look at it, slides are great fun!

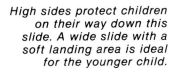

High sides protect children on their way down this slide. A wide slide with a soft landing area is ideal for the younger child.

This more traditional "flat" slide is supported on the high end by a recycled wooden spool. ▶

Rain or shine, the plastic-
covered dome provides a
play area.

Polyhedron Hill

(Courtesy of San Francisco Community Design Center)

Cover the dome's skeletal framework with 6 ml polyethylene plastic to create a unique "glass" house.

Domes to Climb into. Hills to Climb onto.

The completed Polyhedron Hill.

A Play-Car Kids Can Make!

Cardboard does it again, and
half the fun is in the
paint job!

You can use these soft, foam-filled shapes together to produce a variety of exciting and safe obstacle courses and building structures. (Courtesy Skill Development Equipment Co.)

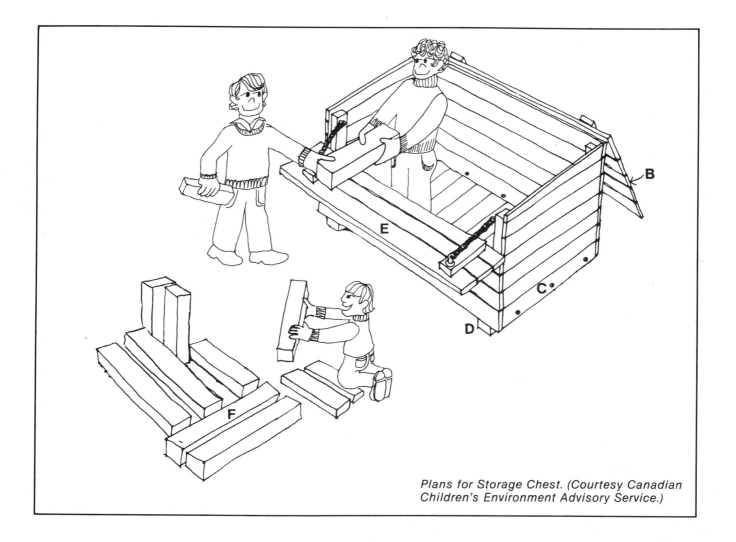

Plans for Storage Chest. (Courtesy Canadian Children's Environment Advisory Service.)

Swedish Blocks and Storage Chest

A. Chest 5'0'' (1500 mm) long, 3'0'' (900 mm) deep, 3'0'' (900 mm) wide. Must be treated with exterior finish and could have padlock.

B. Double hinged lid flat against back when not in use.

C. Drain holes.

D. Raisers approximately 2''x4'' (38x90mm).

E. Drop down front for clambering in and playing "store". Support with chains and heavy duty hinges.

F. For blocks cut lengths of 3''x6'' (65x140 mm) hardwood:
   24 @ 4' (1200 mm) long,
   24 @ 2' (600 mm) long,
   169 @ 1' (300 mm) long,
   Round all edges. Finish blocks with a mixture of good, heavy duty, hardwood floor sealer plus colored oil stain (all blocks to be the same color). When dry remove excess on surface of blocks with fine steel wool.

BLOCKS

Young children absorb a staggering number of facts from many sources every waking hour of their lives. Large, hollow-block building is a medium through which children can build environments for playing out their understanding of the world and its inherent features.

Large blocks are truly versatile. Children can shape them into roads, houses with high walls or rooms laid-out in intricate patterns. They can carry blocks, sit on them, stand on them and use them as cargo for wagons. Blocks encourage balancing, crawling, lifting, climbing, and jumping. The importance of large, hollow-block play for youngsters cannot be overstated.

Children seldom build structures with preconceived notions of what the finished space will look like. Their ideas are continually evolving and changing as they build. Consequently, children need lots of blocks and other loose materials (for example, planks for bridges, roofs and benches) to meet their demands. Many specialists in child development believe that adequate numbers of large, hollow blocks plus loose materials, are all the props preschoolers need for stimulating play.

Replacing, repairing and constantly adding new loose materials are well worth the effort in terms of child development and high sustained play value. If you intend to paint these props, be sure to use the same color. Most adults resist using one color for all props, probably thinking in terms of the old cliche: a child loves bright colors. Actually, in this case, bright colors lower the play value. If the hollow blocks, boards, boxes and barrels are all one practical color, they become modules of one another. This helps to eliminate situations in which children try to "hog" all of the orange ones, etc.

Collecting and painting recycled materials takes little effort. Building large, hollow blocks, however, will require some time and energy on your part. The blocks are best constructed from hardwood and the pieces joined with white carpenter's glue and 2" finishing nails. Round all edges for safety's sake. Finish the blocks with a mixture of heavy-duty hardwood floor sealer and colored oil stain. Use the same color stain on all the blocks to produce a modular effect. Be certain to leave two ends open "or cut in hand-holds," for easy gripping. Sizes of blocks may vary, but two popular sets include blocks of the following dimensions:

SET ONE

Squares	11"x11"x5½"
Rectangles	22"x11"x5½"
Rectangles	5½"x11"x5½"

SET TWO

Rectangles	24"x12"x6"
Squares	12"x12"x6"
Squares	24"x 6"x6"

A total of twenty blocks for one child, thirty blocks for two children, and fifty blocks for three or more children are recommended minimums. Blocks with the largest dimensions should be most plentiful to insure sturdy play structures.

When not in use, blocks can be stacked in the corner of a play area. Or they can be loaded on a dolly or in a crate mounted on casters for storage and easy transport from area to area. The Children's Environments Advisory Service of Canada has designed a highly functional, permanent storage space for blocks temporarily retired from active use. This unique storage chest is five feet long, three feet deep and three feet wide. The double-hinged top lies flat against the back to discourage its use except for locking up. The drop-down front allows for easy entrance and encourages the chest's use as a playhouse when the blocks are in constant use and being stored elsewhere. The front is supported with chains and heavy-duty hinges. The entire chest rests on two 2x4's and has drain holes around the bottom edge. (See page 97.)

MODULAR BUILDING KITS

Modular building kits, such as Tinkertoys, Leggos and Erector Sets can fill hours of creative play time. The great beauty of these pop-and-twist-together units is that they're easy to work with and inspire novel designs. The average child is capable of creating helicopters, cars, skyscrapers, submarines and windmills (to suggest only a few possibilities) with a modular building kit.

With a few wooden connectors and several lengths of wooden or aluminum doweling, you can create a giant building set for the eight to eleven-year-olds in your household. Cut a length of 2"x2" pine into 2" lengths to form the connectors. Drill a ½" diameter hole ½" deep in each face of the pine connectors. Make the connecting rods out of ½" wood dowels in lengths of two and three feet.

Boys and girls can create large play spaces with this system much in the same way Tinkertoys work. The spaces can be enclosed with individual pieces of canvas cut to size (2'x3', 3'x3', 2'x2'). Stitch hems along opposite sides of the canvas sections, thus providing room for the dowels to slip through and hold the canvas panels in place. Or the entire structure can be quickly and economically blanketed with a canvas or plastic tarp.

Large, modular building kits are commercially available. Some have sections that snap together, are joined by x-point joiners, or fit together like plastic plumbing. Units such as these are easy for children to assemble and encourage limitless creative play. (Courtesy Constructive Playthings Co.)

(Courtesy of Childcraft)

(Courtesy Constructive Playthings)

99

By combining these bridges and ladders, kids build their own opportunities for large muscle development through swinging, balancing and climbing. (Courtesy of Constructive Playthings Co.)

BALE HOUSES

Would you like a modular playhouse that can enrich your garden once it has outlived its usefulness as a playhouse? That's exactly the type of structure you can put together in less than fifteen minutes with scarcely more than ten bales of straw.

Jim Kent of Sonama, California, puts one up on "Kid's Day", a special yearly occasion when his family and friends meet for an old-fashioned picnic. According to Jim, this simple playhouse is a favorite with kids of all ages.

Jim's playhouse has a sturdy five-bale foundation laid out in the shape of a pentagon. On top are four additional bales. A single bale forms the pinnacle with an old wooden pallet acting as the roof.

The size and shape of a straw-bale house is limited solely by the number of bales available and your imagination. Jim warns, though, that if you stack the straw four levels or higher, it's best to secure the bales by firmly driving a long wooden or metal stake through them and into the ground.

Once the playhouse is up, you and the youngsters can continue following Jim's advice and cool off in a homemade wading pool. A plastic tarp or ground cover, sandwiched between two or

Bales of straw are the modular building blocks for this playhouse. In Rabat, Morocco, larger versions of this structure dot the countryside, housing many families year round. (Courtesy Jim Kent.)

three rows of stacked railroad ties, works miracles on a muggy, summer afternoon.

Gardeners in particular will appreciate this playhouse as much as the kids. After a year of use, you can mulch the structure directly into your vegetable patch.

DOMES

In recent years, domes have excited architectural imagination, perhaps because a sphere is the most perfect shape. Designed by R. Buckminister Fuller in 1948 after observing nature and applying its principles to man made structures, the geodesic dome is simply a geometric joining of triangles in tension in such a way that a minimum of materials covers a maximum area.

Domes are cropping up everywhere these days, not only as homes, but in structures as diverse as college dormatories, ski lodges, churches and restaurants. Why not a dome playhouse, too?

Dome-raising requires a bit more precision than most of the other play spaces described in *Successful Playhouses.* Therefore, I strongly advise you to play around with models before getting down to actual construction. Use toothpicks as the struts and fresh, shelled green peas (or small lumps of modeling clay) as the connecting hubs of your model. Once the peas have dried, they'll form a tight bond, holding the toothpicks securely in place.

Domes come in many shapes and sizes. Some are made of triangles with sides of equal lengths; others have triangles with sides of differing lengths. Domes with faces of two differing lengths are called two-frequency domes. With several successful models to your credit, try your hand at putting together a playhouse dome. What follows is a plan for a two-frequency dome made from wood dowels and home-fabricated surgical tubing or garden hose connecting hubs.

The materials you'll need are: 26' garden hose or surgical tubing (½" ID); 26 - ¼"x1" carriage bolts; 26 wing nuts; 52 washers; 30 - ½" dowels, 36" long; and 35 - ½" dowels, 31¾" long.

The only tools that are required: a drill and a handsaw.

Building domes with solid hubs is a difficult task. Cutting slots into the ends of struts so they extend away from the hubs with the right angle

Domes made from sturdy materials make excellent climbing structures, while those less sturdy can be used to climb through or under.

can be a painstaking process. Hubs made from thick surgical tubing or garden hose make it simple because the hub itself bends naturally to form the angle.

Cut the hose or tubing into 4" - 4½" lengths. Drill a hole through the center of each section large enough for the ¼"x1" carriage bolt to fit through. With a washer in place next to the bolt, push three pieces of hose onto the unit. The warmer and more malleable the hose, the easier this job becomes. Slip a second washer onto the exposed end of the bolt and fasten down with a wing nut. If the hose is too thick, you may want to use a longer bolt. Just be sure the bolt doesn't protrude too far beyond the hub and become a safety hazard.

Domes are built from the top down. Start by inserting five 31¾" long dowels into a hub, forming a star. Lay this unit on the ground. It will end up being the top-center of the dome. Now make five separate equilateral triangles from the 36" doweling and hubs. Position each of these finished triangles around the top-center unit and attach at the hubs. Pick the top-center up slightly to make the connections.

Construct five more stars from the shorter dowels. Connect these to the dome as shown. Again, someone will have to lift the top-center piece

slightly in order to make all connections. Build five more triangles and fasten them, end-to-end, with the first set of triangles. Connect the loose star ends to the hubs at the triangles. As you go along, you'll have to remove hubs from the ends of triangles that match up with triangles that already have hubs in place.

Finish your 5'2" high, 9'9" diameter dome by adding the remaining five 31¾" dowels to the open spaces around the perimeter.

News of a dome-raising spreads quickly. Let the rapidly growing crowd of kids cover the structure with newspaper or corrugated paper to create a cozy and private playhouse. Coat the dome with shellac for greater rigidity and weatherproofing and cut in windows and doors. Or cover the entire structure with 6 ml polyethylene plastic sheeting for an avante-garde "glass" playhouse.

Finishing the inside of full-scale domes often is a tedious task. Paneling the curved walls and installing cupboards are difficult chores. Your children won't have any of these problems with their play dome. A touch of poster paint on canvas or paper-covered structures might be in order. Domes are great surfaces on which to paint "3-D" murals.

Once the kids' dome is complete, you will all want to sit back and admire your creative efforts. A simple stool that will serve this purpose can be made from a discarded cardboard tube and a piece of scrap tri-wall cardboard. Tubes can be picked up, usually free, from rug and carpet outlets as well as from paper companies. Give a few of these local industries a call to see what's available.

Use a common hand saw to cut the tube to the desired height. Next cut a circle of cardboard with a diameter large enough to sit on comfortably. Tape or glue the circular disc onto the tube. That's all there is to it.

Two youngsters can assemble this dome in less than 15 minutes. When not in use, the dome can be disassembled and stored in the corner of a small closet. Domes made from lightweight materials such as the dowels used in this structure are not for climbing.

SOLAR COOKER

On sunny days, it might be fun to have a barbecue by the dome. But instead of using a traditional barbecue next to your unique dome, prepare a meal on a non-traditional, "kid-size" solar cooker.

The materials you'll need are: 1-28"x43" poster board; 1-1"x3"x8" block of wood; 1, tin can (6" diameter); flat black paint; nails, white carpenter's glue; masking tape; aluminum foil; and a glass bowl or glass lid.

The tools you'll need are: scissors, metal shears, and a hammer.

INSTRUCTIONS FOR ASSEMBLING SOLAR COOKER

1. Copy the pattern on the following page, onto a sheet of poster board measuring 28"x43". Cut out the pattern using a pair of heavy scissors or sharp mat knife.

2. Trim a piece of aluminum foil to the same dimensions of the flat, cardboard shape. Now carefully spread white glue on one side of the cardboard, then attach the foil, shiny side up.

3. With the foil facing inward, bend the cardboard into a cone (the cone will not be completely symmetrical). Before you tape together the ends of the cone, check that the 6" diameter can fits snugly through the small opening of the cone.

4. Remove the can from the cone. With a pair of metal shears, trim the tin can down to a height of 2". Leave two "rabbit ears" diagonally across from each other. Now paint the can flat black, inside and out. When the paint dries, nail the black can to a block of wood measuring 1"x3"x8".

5. Position the small end of the reflecting cone over the tin can. The cone should rest securely on the block of wood. Your solar cooker is complete.

6. Aim the cooker at the sun by propping up the cooker in a cardboard box. Wrap your meal in aluminum foil (for best results, paint the foil flat black on the outside only). Place the uncooked food in the tin can, cover with a clear glass bowl or lid and sit back and enjoy the aroma.

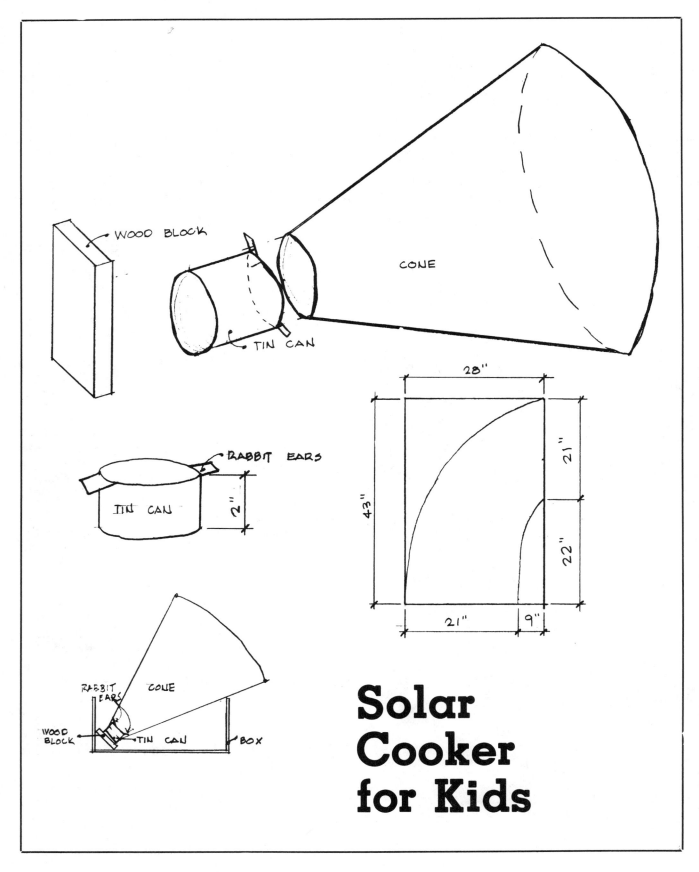

WOOD BLOCK

CONE

TIN CAN

RABBIT EARS

TIN CAN

2"

28"

43"

21"

22"

21"

9"

RABBIT EARS

CONE

WOOD BLOCK

TIN CAN

BOX

Solar Cooker for Kids

Your meal will cook at 240°F and soon you'll be eating a sun-cooked dinner.

SUNDIAL

Domes definitely belong out in the sun. It seems only natural that children playing in domes should learn how to tell time, not with watches, but with the sun. A simple sundial will not only help them keep track of the good time they're having, but also teach them quite a bit about their home planet and the ball of fire that feeds it.

There's no magic involved in constructing a functional sundial, simply drive a stick of any height into the ground. Every hour, on the hour, drive a second, smaller stake into the ground at the end of the shadow cast by the first stake. Mark the time on the smaller stake for reference. By sundown, you will have created a semi-circle of sticks, each at equal intervals and resembling half a clock face.

Your kids can build a more traditional sundial of wood or cardboard. The shadow caster is cut in the shape of a triangle whose base angle is the same as your area's latitude (consult an almanac). The longest edge of the triangle — the edge facing skywards — should point to the North Star.

Mount this triangular shadow caster on a base and mark off the hours as the shadow falls.

POLYHEDRON HILL

Polyhedron Hill is even more impressive than its name. This structure is one of the most unusual and exciting play spaces in existence. It was originally designed by architect David Gast of the Community Design Center of San Francisco, California. Gast and the Center came up with the idea for a portable play space in response to San Francisco neighborhood requests for improved recreational facilities. Their concept of a portable play area was first unveiled at the National Association of Architects in 1968 where it received an award of $2500 from Mrs. Lyndon B. Johnson.

Polyhedron Hill was designed for entire neighborhoods. But, its versatility makes it easily adaptable to your backyard. The Hill is a component system from which an infinite number of different configurations can be made. The structure can be readily adapted to meet different design critera such as site and space limitations, and number and age of children (the Hill was designed primarily for kids 5-12).

Models of Polyhedron Hill made from cardboard will help you and your children create a Hill best suited to your backyard. (Courtesy San Francisco Community Design Center.)

The Amazing Polyhedron Hill

(Courtesy San Francisco Community Design Center.)

The basic building blocks of the Polyhedron Hill are flat, hexagonal (6-sided) and half-hexagonal panels. These are joined together by hinges into polyhedra (many-sided solid shapes) called truncated octhedrons, and stacked to form hills for climbing over and tunneling through. Slides, bridges, mirrors, chalk boards, colored murals, benches and trees can be added to the Hill. The result is a miniature play world that triggers the imagination of children, a world that allows for all types of physical, social, creative and quiet play.

The best way to gain an understanding of how the system functions is to make scale models. Cut a large number of hexagons and half hexagons out of poster board (1½" on each side). Join eight hexagons together with tape in the pattern pictured on page 105. Make a number of these units and stack them in different configurations. Add additional half-hexagonal and hexagonal panels for ground level benches and bridges.

When you have a design that pleases you and the kids, determine the materials you will need for construction. Each hexagonal panel has either 3, 4, 5 or 6 sides with connectors to adjoining panels. Use the chart (see below) to figure the number of full hexagonal panels you'll need.

The quantity and type of materials differ according to individual design needs. What follows are some suggestions from the staff of the Community Design Center.

Connectors on:		Panels without Foot Slots	Panels with Foot Slots	Total
	3 edges			
	4 edges			
	5 edges			
	6 edges			
	Total			

Chart for calculating no. panels. (Courtesy San Francisco Community Design Center.)

PANELS

Use ¾" A-B exterior plywood in 4'x8' sheets. You get three full hexagonal panels or 9 half-hexagonal panels from one sheet. In lighter use situations, it should be possible to use ⅝" or even ¼" plywood. Interior grade plywood can be used for indoor use.

EDGE CONNECTORS

The Center uses hinges as the edge connectors — Stanley RD741 3½"x3½" with USP finish (bonderized, prime painted) or equivalent. You need one pair of hinges per connecting edge. Phillips head screws (¾"x8", zinc chromate) and teenuts (size 8-32) are used to attach the hinges to the panels (12 of each per pair of hinges). The hinges make it possible to easily assemble the panels or disassemble them for moving by simply knocking out the hinge pins.

BASIC BUILDING INSTRUCTIONS

1. Cut out the hexagonal and half-hexagonal panels from the plywood sheets (easiest with a radial or table saw).

2. Cut out the foot slots in the hexagonal panels that will be in a sloping position and serve as climbing surfaces (saber saw).

3. Round the corners and edges of the panels (belt sander).

4. Fill all surface and edge faults with plastic wood and then sand.

5. Make a poster board or masonite hexagonal template for accurate drilling of hinge mounting holes. Accurately drilled holes will correct for slight variations in cut panels. Center this template on the panels and mark the hole locations.

6. Drill the $7/32$" hinge holes (electric or hand drill).

7. Hammer the teenuts into the holes opposite the side the hinge half is to be mounted on.

8. Screw the hinge halves onto the panels.

9. Paint the panels. Use one coat of primer followed by two coats of heavy-duty exterior primer.

10. Assemble the play structure by knocking in the hinge pins. It will often be necessary to adjust the spacing between the hinges by tapping with a hammer.

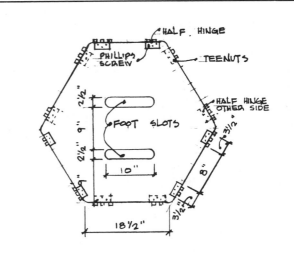

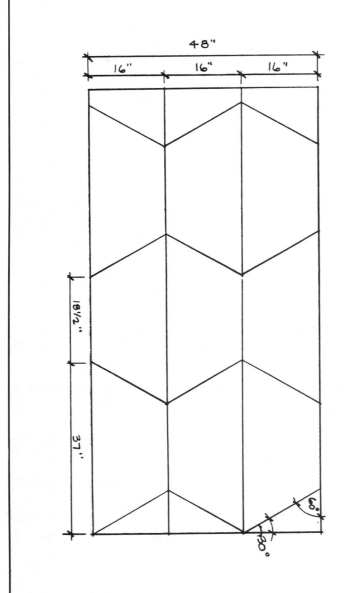

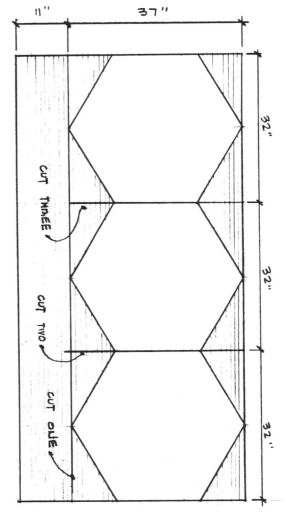

Diagram of full and half panels. (Courtesy San Francisco Community Design Center.)

TRUNCATED TETRAHEDRON

The Polyhedron Hill is a climbing and tunneling haven for kids 5-12. The Hill's smaller cousin, the Truncated Tetrahedron, is a good introduction to climbing for preschoolers. With the addition of side paneling, this small structure converts to a cozy, enclosed space.

A truncated tetrahedron is a 3-D, six-sides-of-the-same-length-with-the-ends-cut-off-triangle. You'll need six equal lengths of 4"x6" lumber with 55° angles cut at both ends (angles face the same side). These sides are joined together with four one-inch exterior grade plywood end plates.

The completed truncated tetrahedron is an odd looking duck, almost prehistoric. But it brings into play your child's entire body. Climbing up and proceeding around and through the Truncated Tetrahedron is a combination of slithering, crawling, chinning, pulling and pushing. The Tetrahedron is a very functional contemporary dinosaur.

The truncated tetrahedron is made of six lengths of heavy-duty lumber joined at the ends by 1" thick hexagonal plywood endplates.

Miter the ends of each side to 55°. You can build the structure large or small, depending on the length of the sides; regardless of side length, all timber ends must be cut at 55° for proper assembly. Bolt the ends of the timber to the plywood plates using 3" lag screws.

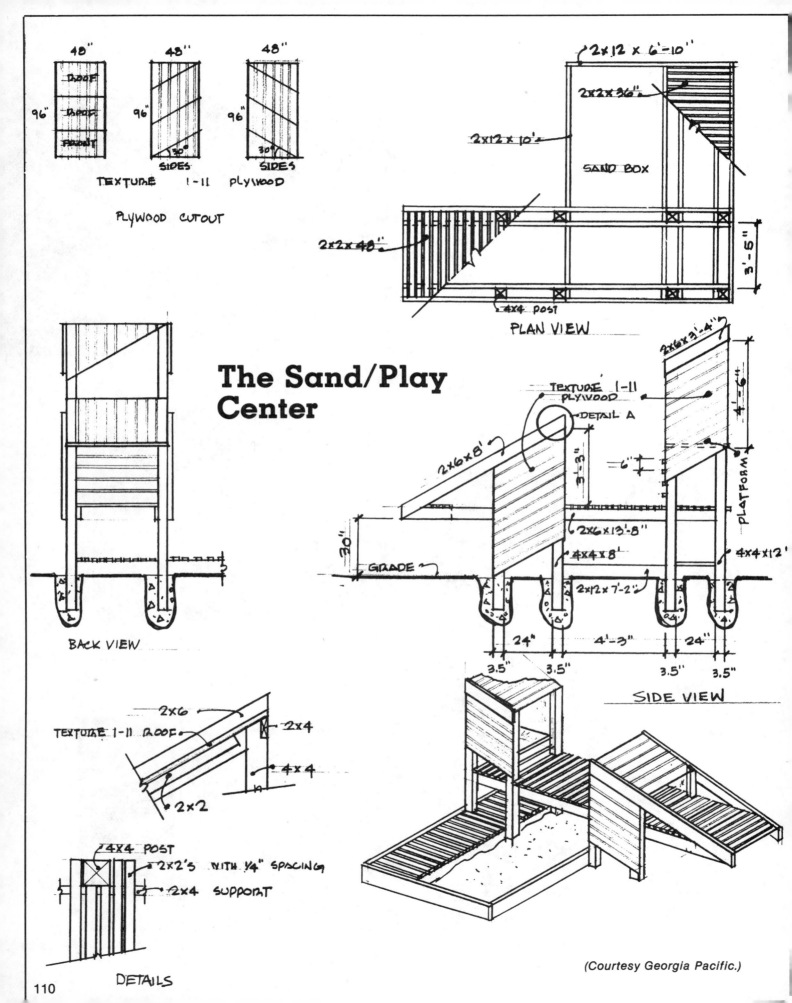

48"

48"

48"

ROOF

ROOF

FRONT

96"

96"

96"

30°

30°

SIDES

SIDES

TEXTURE 1-11 PLYWOOD

PLYWOOD CUTOUT

2x12 x 6'-10"

2x2x36"

2x12 x 10'

SAND BOX

2x2 x 48"

3'-5"

4x4 POST

PLAN VIEW

The Sand/Play Center

BACK VIEW

2x6x3'-4"

TEXTURE 1-11 PLYWOOD

DETAIL A

4'-6"

2x6x8'

3-3"

6"

PLATFORM

30"

2x6x13'-8"

GRADE

4x4x8'

4x4x12'

2x12 x 7'-2"

24"

4'-3"

24"

3.5"

3.5"

3.5"

3.5"

SIDE VIEW

2x6

TEXTURE 1-11 ROOF

2x4

4x4

2x2

4x4 POST

2x2's WITH 1/4" SPACING

2x4 SUPPORT

DETAILS

(Courtesy Georgia Pacific.)

5 Sand and Water Play

Alisa, Ian, John and Penny, all four-year-olds, are busily getting lunch ready for the opening of their new restaurant. Twenty feet away, four-year-old Sara and her best buddy, Linda, recreate a fierce battle between prehistoric dinosaurs. The environment that these two make-believe archeologists have created for the battle — swamps laden with quicksand and prolific vegetation — is remarkably similar to the pictures in the big book the girls have just gone through.

Both groups of children are playing and working out their fantasies with sand and water. These two versatile substances promote instant dramatic play among children. Dramatic play is important to the psychological growth of young children. It provides a channel through which kids act out and assimilate important events. Children also are able to more easily experience intimate, interpersonal communications during sand and water play, thereby enhancing their social growth. Intellectually, dramatic play revolving around sand and water offers a means of organizing impressions at a time when manipulation of abstract symbols is just developing. No wonder, then, that researchers of child development report that raw materials such as sand and water help kids develop into happy, healthy individuals who are better able to cope with the world.

SAND

Sand is a plastic substance. It can become flour, concrete, steel, sugar, asphalt or whatever the child desires. The first step for making the most of this "transmutable" material in your backyard is to contain it properly. Make sure that the fine particles cannot blow out of the sandy area into children's eyes. Sink the sandbox into the ground or build a lip around it. Since water is often an integral part of sand play, see to it that the area is well drained.

A very simple container, especially well suited to tiny tots of two and under, is one made of double or triple wall cardboard. Use a sheet of cardboard with minimum dimensions of 4'x4'. Draw a line parallel to, and one foot in from, each edge. Now cut out the four small squares formed by the intersections of those lines at each corner. Simply fold up the sides and secure with duct tape to form the sandbox. If the younger ones will be using water, line the box with a large sheet of 6 ml polyethylene plastic. A sturdy sandbox of the same basic design can be made from lumber or plywood. To insure proper drainage, mount the wooden box on 2x4 legs and drill drainage holes in the bottom for water that might accumulate.

The sand you put into these and other boxes should be a clean washed construction variety, one that can be moulded during play activities. The minimum depth ranges from 12"-18" (your kids will need at least that much sand for satisfying digging).

Georgia-Pacific has designed a sand play-center that many backyards can accommodate. The play-center, complete with sandbox and look-out tower, is easy to construct by following the diagrams on the opposite page.

MATERIALS YOU'LL NEED

3	4'x8'x⅝''; G-P Texture 1-11 siding
4	4''x4''x12' lumber
4	4''x4''x8' lumber
2	4''x4''x2' lumber
2	2''x6''x3'4'' lumber
2	2''x6''x8' lumber
2	2''x6''x13'8'' lumber
3	2''x12''x10' lumber
2	2''x12''x7'2'' lumber

2	2"x6"x17¾" lumber
3	2"x6"x4' lumber
108	2"x2"x4' (55') lumber
70	2"x2"x3' (22') lumber
2	2"x6"x33" lumber
2	2"x2"x41" lumber
3	2"x4"x41" lumber
3	4"x6"x8' lumber
1	4"x6"x6' lumber
8	4"x6"x12' lumber
4	2"x2"x2' lumber
1	6'1" hardwood dowel

The tools you'll need are: posthole digger, shovel, hammer, wrenches, cross cut saw, and drill.

In the planning stages, take extra care to treat lumber that will come into contact with cement or ground with wood preservative. Once you and the children have agreed on a building site, follow the basic plan by first installing the 4"x4" vertical supports, making sure to allow 24 inches of depth for each hole. Cement and let dry. While you're waiting for the cement to set, measure and level the 4'x10' sandbox area.

Now you're ready to make the deck supports. For the upper deck, nail the two 2"x6"x13'8" deck beams into place, drill and bolt securely. Using ¼" wood spacers, lay down the 4' pieces of 2"x2" decking and nail.

For the lower deck and sandbox area, bolt the precut 10 foot 2"x2" to the base of the vertical supports. Lap the end of the sandbox under the deck with the 2"x2"x7'2" deck support. Lay in the 2"x2"x3' decking and nail with galvanized nails.

For the lookout platform, bolt the 2"x6"x33" supports into place 2'6" above the upper deck.

Lay in the 2"x2" decking and nail. The top 2"x6" braces are cut at 30°.

Add the precut side panels (cut at 60°) and front panels. Next, bolt into place the three 2"x2"x4' ladder rungs. You're almost there. Nail the 2"x2" roof braces into place and nail on the 3"x4" Texture 1-11 roof panels. Finish off with stain or paint.

The Canadian Children's Environments Advisory Service has developed plans for another well-designed sandpit. Their sandpit has a built-in "cake table" to help prevent overspill. According to Polly Hill, Service Advisor, another deterrent to overflow is to round the outside edge of the pit with the addition of a half log, curved side up, attached to the wood timber sides. If bricks or concrete are used, this curved edge is easily formed around the pit's perimeter. However you do it, avoid flat outside edges because they encourage "cake baking" and spilling.

"The level of the sand below the edge (at least 12") also prevents blowing", Hill points out. "You may need to add a step down for little children. Hedging or another type of wind screen may be necessary for some sites. Cobblestones or flat paving stones around the sandpit help take sand off the feet and improve the appearance. If cats are a real problem, nylon netting that allows rain and purifying sun rays through can be stretched over the sand when not in use (never completely cover as sand will go rancid!). A hand rake or scooper permanently stored nearby is a still simpler solution."

A special note about sandpit drainage. When the ground water seepage is good, the base of the pit can be brick with gravel underneath. When seepage is poor or the water table is high, dig a dry well or install a drain line.

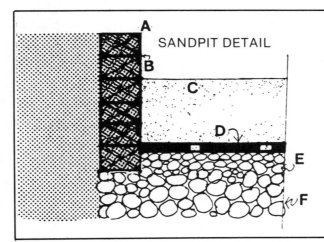

SANDPIT DETAIL

A. Round all exposed edges.
B. 6"x8" (140x190 mm) or 8"x8" (190x190 mm) wood timber. Treat with preservative and bolt or dowel together. Retaining wall to be 12" (300 mm) minimum above level of sand.
C. Sand 1'0" to 1'6" (300-450 mm) deep.
D. Concrete slabs under sand spaced to permit water drainage.
For sandy or gravelly soil:
E. 4" (100 mm) of ¾" (20 mm) crushed stone.
F. 12" (300 mm) of 1½" (40 mm) granular material.
For clay soil:
G. Drain tile to drainage outlet (e.g., storm sewer).
Note: Sand pit can be a free form. Then make retaining wall of wood or concrete with same drainage detail. Use smooth stones along top edge to give natural look.

(Courtesy of The Canadian Children's Environment Advisory Service)

Build a Sand Pit

(Courtesy Canadian Children's Environments Advisory Service.)

SAND TABLE

Sandboxes allow children to climb into the sand and are one of the best ways to make this remarkable substance (sand) available for play. When building a sandbox isn't feasible because of space limitations, your next best alternative is a sand table. A sand table is a table that contains sand.

Sand tables that require children to stand up should be approximately 22" high for kids five and younger. If the table is a sit-down model, then it should be no higher than 16" from the ground.

When one or more children are playing at a sand table, the limited area of the sand may give way to territorial conflicts. An area large enough for the activities of one child in the sand table is 18 lineal inches (in larger sandboxes, the minimum area is 28 square feet — a circle with an approximate radius of three feet). Kids confined to wheel chairs can get to the sand more easily if half circles are cut in the table big enough for the child and wheel chair to move into.

Kids in wheelchairs need easy access to sand tables.

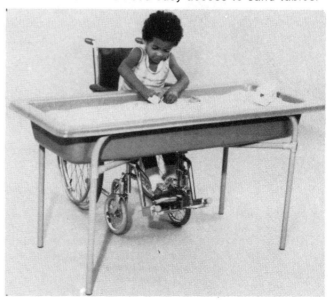

A sandbox doesn't have to be a sandbox to be a sandbox.

Young children need protection from overexposure to the sun. An A-frame (2x4's covered with pegboard) provides adequate shade in this sandbox. Note the sand cover leaning against the frame.

MAKE-BELIEVE

Add a splash of water and the versatility of sand increases immensely. Water and sand together lend themselves to imaginary "cooking". Give your kids old pie pans, muffin tins, cookie cutters, sieves and rolling pins to encourage creative play.

You can help them make their own kitchen appliances quite easily. Orange crates, apple boxes or handmade cardboard tables, stoves, cabinets and chairs will lend themselves quite well to any imaginary kitchen. For example, a stove, cupboard, refrigerator and sink can be made from discarded cantelope crates. One crate forms the skeletal frame while slats from another crate fill in the spaces between ribs, making a solid-looking appliance. Use inverted tart pans for burners and cookie molds for dials that actually turn. Add a plastic dish pan to the sink for holding water. For added realism, hinge doors and add shelves to the cupboard and refrigerator.

Encourage diversity in role-playing with additional props: old plastic and metal gears, pill bottles, boxes, a plumber's helper, wheels, mugs, balances, cans, hoses, sponges, springs, mirrors and cardboard tubes.

A wide variety of props is important for a child's intellectual development. Props, such as those already mentioned, require fine muscle skills for proper handling. Many of these same skills also are used in performing intellectual tasks: grasping and holding pencils for writing, finger coordination for using scissors, hand and eye coordination for pressing buttons to turn teaching machines on and off. The state of "reading readiness," for example, is highly dependent on mastering these muscle skills. Stop and think for a moment about the mechanics of reading: holding the book steady, turning the pages, and following the lines with your eyes. Youngsters who master these prerequisite motor skills will be physically prepared for reading. And what better way to learn these skills than through natural and spontaneous play.

Here's a list of even more "instant toys" to have available: aluminum foil; ball bearings; beads; cellophane; chains; clay; clock springs; costume jewelry; hat boxes; leather remnants; linoleum; marbles; wallpaper; photographs; phonograph records; pine cones; pocket-books; pipe cleaners; rope; rug yarn; sandpaper; sea shells; spools; tin cans; clothespins; zippers; tongue depressors; tin foil; wire hairpins; wire paperclips.

MUD

Mud makes an excellent toy. That's right — MUD! The term may cause many parents to cringe with fear. Mud is one of the most natural mediums for children to work with. The tactile sensations alone are hard to duplicate with other substances. And every child occasionally needs a mud hole to climb into. As a consenting parent, your major duty will be to watch out for your children's health (no sticking heads under, please) and to have dry clothes nearby. Otherwise, the best role you can play is that of observer.

Basically the same kinds of loose materials used in sand and water play are suited to mud. Extras might include long planks for bridge building; big rocks for pushing around; buckets for hauling the thick brew; and, serving trays for drying mud people, animals and food. Don't forget short-handled shovels for the initial work of digging the mud hole.

Digging is an activity suited to children of all ages. Kids uncover all kinds of secrets in each shovelful including rocks, worms, roots or an occasional piece of broken pottery. Digging also provides a sense of pride and accomplishment, especially when excavating a "big" hole. Be sure, though, to restrict these potentially big, muddy holes to a corner of the yard where they won't interfere with your gardening and relaxation.

WATER

Take away the dirt and the sand, and you're left holding a bucket of water. By contributing opportunities to experiment and explore, water play stimulates intellectual development. Another plus for water play is the therapeutic effect it has on children, especially beneficial for hyperactive kids.

With a bit of luck, you may be able to find an old produce table from a grocery store and convert it into a backyard water table. Check all seams to insure they are water-tight. Fill the table with three to five inches of water, an adequate depth for the needs of most children. If the water table is on asphalt or concrete, the addition of wheels or rollers will add to the unit's versatility. If the kids aren't in bathing suits or old clothes, have water smocks available. Inexpensive smocks can be made from old slickers.

Water tables don't have to be as elaborate as produce tables. Any container that holds three to five inches will bring pleasure and learning. On a

This completely transparent trough adds an extra dimension to water play. Being able to see under water allows youngsters greater room for exploration and experimentation. (Courtesy Childcraft.)

smaller scale, use an old plastic baby bath. Filled with corks, funnels, measuring cups, spoons, egg beaters, straws (the large plastic ones are best), sponges, pill bottles, plastic lemons, clear plastic tubing, food coloring, measuring cups, plastic containers of various sizes and shapes and plastic syringes, these miniature water tables provide as much fascination and developmental benefits as their larger versions.

Other alternatives for water tables include plastic dish pans and wading pools. On a much larger and fashionable scale, hot tubs, when filled with the aforementioned water toys and with an adult in attendance, provide the same exciting experiences.

WATER PUMPS

One of the problems that traditionally accompanies water play, particularly when there is an outlet nearby, is waste. Kids tend to let the water run when there is no need. A pump is a great solution to this wasteful problem. The water ceases to flow once the pumping action stops. A pump's not only fun, but educational. It demonstrates rather dramatically the process of cause and effect.

You can find a variety of pumps in your local hardware store or machine shop. When you buy one, ask for specific installation instructions. Otherwise, here are some very general installation tips: 1. Put the pump on a concrete slab, reinforced and textured to provide a nonslip surface for wet feet; 2. If you're in an area that does not have wells, hook the pump to an existing outlet. To insure the flow of water only after the children have cranked the handle one full time, install a limited-flow valve. The valve will act as a "tap". Limited-flow valves can be found in most plumbing supply houses or hardware stores; 3. Keep the area around the waterplay area and pump from becoming a swamp with adequate drainage. A bucket punched with holes, filled with loose gravel and sunk into the ground at the foot of the pump is usually quite sufficient.

BACKYARD STREAM

When space and facilities permit, the "ultimate" water table is a play stream you and the kids dig yourselves. A hose-filled stream leads to hours of imaginative water play that promotes constructive and perceptive intellectual development. A

Pumps add an exciting quality to water play. A child, perceiving the cause-effect relationship in the action of the pump, really learns the dynamics of water mechanics. (Courtesy Childcraft.)

stream can be any size and shape, but it must drain to the lowest point. Water should be a maximum of 6" deep and the edge of the stream lined with smooth, flat stones (for permanence, lay the stones in mortar over reinforced concrete or asphalt that covers the bottom of the stream). Whether the stream bed is asphalt or concrete, lay a gravel base to insure that the bed doesn't wash or dissolve away. Remember to install the drain at the lowest point. The outlet should be connected to a dry well or a sewer depending on local building codes. Stopper the hole with a plug attached to the bottom with a chain (a standard bathroom fixture). Add a screw mesh at the top of the drain to prevent clogging.

A bucket filled with water from the stream or from a nearby pump immediately becomes a gallon of paint in a child's mind. With a few old paint brushes, your kids can paint the house, porch, patio, their playhouses and, perhaps, give the family car an extra coat of imaginary, shiny acrylic. Water painting is a satisfying activity for 3-to 8-year-olds. For more detailed painting jobs, the kids can load smaller paint jars (2 oz. coffee or baby food jars) into empty soft drink sixpacks.

After the youngsters have painted the neighborhood with water, why not let them try their hand at "spatter" painting. Cut a hole in the top of a three-gallon ice cream container and cover with a piece of screen fastened down with tape. Use water-colors and an old toothbrush to spatter paper placed below the wire mesh. A stainless steel aquarium or cage lid set on blocks gives an even wider spatter area.

Don't forget about bubbles! Bubble blowing equipment should be standard fare for all water tables. Your kids can make a bubble pipe quite easily from a plastic soda straw. A styrofoam cup makes an excellent container for the bubbly brew which you make from ¾ cups of liquid soap, ¼ cup glycerine and two quarts tap water. Adult supervision is recommended for three-year-olds and under. You may have to teach this age group how to blow out through the straw rather than sucking in. Make an extra bubbler and join the fun!

INSIDE PLAY

The natural place for sand and water play is outside. But that doesn't prohibit you from bringing these two activities indoors. Any indoor sand table can be made from any of the tables already mentioned in this chapter. To prevent damage to tile and hardwood floors, put down a drop cloth or old carpet to absorb the sand. Better yet, substitute corn meal for sand. Corn meal is much softer and appropriate for indoor use. Make indoor, rainy day play as much fun as outdoor activities with the addition of a few kitchen utensils, sand screens (made by securing different sizes of wire mesh to simple wooden frames), pails, scoops, funnels (cut in-half a discarded plastic container with a molded handle approximately three inches below the handle, to create a scoop/funnel combination) and magnifying lenses to take closer looks at the corn meal and surfaces of the toys.

STORAGE

Rotate all the kids' props. Keep some of the materials out on the shelves while you "store away" the others. When it looks as though the children could use some variety, take away the little-used props and replace with "new" materials. *Important note to parents of pre-schoolers:* limit the actual number of props kept on the open shelves. Young children are easily overwhelmed by too many choices. Youngsters also find it a more manageable task to shelve a few materials when compared to replacing mounds of props.

Of course, your kids will need a storage area for

Pieces in this storage unit fit together with notches; no other fastenings are required.

all the water and sand toys, whether indoors or outdoors. A simple storage space can be made from plywood particle board or double-wall card-board (indoor use only). Use the photo above as a guide to cutting materials. Make four uprights and five shelves. Add a solid back piece for stability. This storage space is ideal because it provides easy access to all the materials stored on it. The main purpose of storage is to separate objects and make them easily accessible. For this reason, place the storage unit as close as possible to the areas where the kids will be using the materials.

After a time, it may become necessary to construct a storage shed (all those water and sand toys add up!). A separate shed is far better than storing loose materials in a regular play structure. And unless you've designed the storage shed to sub as a playhouse, don't encourage the kids to use it as a playhouse. Another consideration to keep in mind is to keep the shed shallow. The deeper the space, the more difficulty children have getting at specific items. Before long, the shed will degrade into a junk pile. During winter months, see to it that the storage area is raised on pads. This precaution will prevent ground snow from interfering with opening and closing the door and will keep damaging water off the materials inside.

A SPECIAL NOTE TO PARENTS

There are lots of reasons for giving your kids access to mud, sand and water. Some of those reasons have been covered in this chapter. "But are those messy things really all that important for my children's development", you still may question. No authority will ever be able to convince you as well as yourself. And the best way to convince yourself is to dig in and explore first-hand.

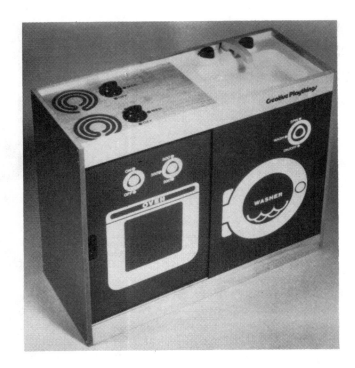

A single unit kitchen center can be made from hardwood and hardboard. This all-in-one kitchen play center includes realistic stove, oven, sink and washing machine. (Courtesy Creative Playthings.)

This play center contains all the appliances normally found in a real kitchen. The kitchen is handcrafted ▶ from hardwood.

Create "Make-Believe" for indoor fun!

No kitchen is complete without cooking utensils. (Courtesy Creative Playthings.)

6
"Kid-Built" Playhouses

All the playhouses described in this book should be "kid-built." If not the actual builders, then your children should act as consultants. Let them help you determine step and rail height, window and door placement, location in the backyard and finishing touches. Remember that what looks good to you may not look so inviting to a rambunctious preschooler or sixth grader.

With a few exceptions, most of the playhouses described have been for outdoor use. But play spaces aren't limited solely to the outside. A simple playhouse that is a lot of fun for three to nine-year-olds to construct is an indoor tent. Blankets, sheets, towels, chairs, couches and/or stools — just about any covering material and piece of furniture in the house — can be used to construct an indoor tent. With the addition of a few safety pins (handled by older kids only), the tent's walls can be fastened down permanently.

When the tent house stays up a few days (when heavy snows and thunderous rains make outside play impossible), I've seen children's creations rival the Winchester Mystery House in size, number of rooms and ingenuity. Doors and secret entrances appear from nowhere, peep holes dot the tent's sides, favorite toys disappear into it's shadowy depths. For some children, building these large, complex structures also provides a genuine feeling of power and escape from the limitations of childhood.

Indoor tents spark a child's imagination. Youngsters are able to act out their fantasies and fears in a safe environment. So, if it's raining outside, and your youngsters are climbing the walls, suggest an indoor tent.

ROOM WEAVING

Another activity for an inside day is room weaving. Keep this one confined to the children's

bedroom. It doesn't take long for young weavers to "tie-up" an entire house! Materials you'll need on hand include little more than string, yarn or small-diameter cord. You might want to show your children how to start by tying one end of the string to an object such as a dresser drawer knob.

Then, they can wrap it around a bed leg and pull it over to the desk. When the kids come to the end of the string or yarn they can fasten it down to something close by or knot-in another length of cord. Room weaving is free-form activity well-suited to a child's spontaneity.

BUILDING BLOCKS

Have available a set of building blocks for additional indoor playhouses. The whole family can make the blocks from either double- and or triple-wall cardboard. Block sizes can vary, but a good size to start with is 10"x10". Glue the block faces together to form a cube. With a little experience, you can help your kids create blocks of any dimension or size.

Building blocks are non-threatening and controllable. For some children, building giant, elaborate structures and then afterwards knocking them down is a way of expressing power and releasing aggression.

CARDBOARD SLIDE

A cardboard slide is another play structure that can be used either inside or outside. The older kids in your family or next door can make it for the younger set.

Portable
Slide of Cardboard
and Dowels

MATERIALS FOR SLIDE

9-3/4"	threaded dowels, 18" long
14	nuts for 3/4" dowel
2	sides, cut from 4x6' triwall
1	slide surface, 7 or 8' by 15" (sliding surface could be made 2 layers thick)
1	cardboard spacer 6" x 15" (or 2 more nuts)

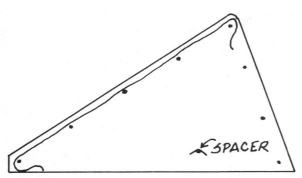

X-ray view: bend sliding surface to fit around dowels. Bind edges with tape.

Clamp 2 sides together & punch holes for rungs.

(Courtesy of the Workshops for Learning Things)

OUTDOOR

The Sierra Madre Community Nursery School in southern California has designed a unique playhouse that kids can continue to build forever because it is never complete. When they're not building, the children can climb around its exposed skeleton. This unusual playhouse is the unfinished frame of a "kid-size" house.

According to Lillian Burke, Director of the School, the frame originally was constructed by one of the preschooler's fathers. The structure can be used by children in a variety of ways and is strong enough to endure a never ending onslaught of hammers and nails. Kids can use whatever materials are available to "complete" the little house. Cardboard, corrugated paper, lumber scraps and acoustical tile make good covering materials.

"When available," Mrs. Burke writes, "we have given the children old radio parts, springs, wire and telephones. Rigging this equipment inside the building stimulates their imagination, not only in construction, but in the dramatic play that emerges. Several times they have hauled blocks to it, 'furnishing the interior'"

Before turning the kids loose, instruct them in the proper use of tools. It may take some practice before the younger ones master the art of hitting a nail squarely on the head or turning a screw into a block of wood. An adult should quietly supervise the young carpenters' efforts once they're on their own.

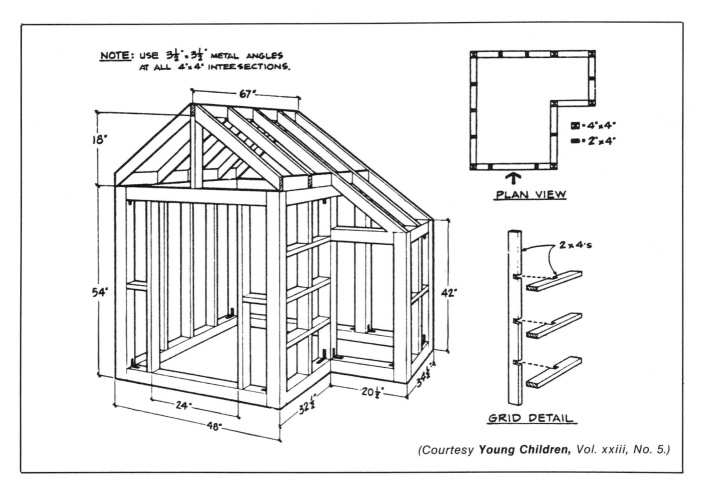

(Courtesy Young Children, Vol. xxiii, No. 5.)

This frame structure gives young carpenters something big and practical to work on. The frame pictured here has survived twelve years of hammering and nailing. (Courtesy Sierra Madra Community Nursery School.)

Once proficient in the use of tools, the children should be able to store their equipment in their own tool chest, just as any master carpenter does. Tool boxes can be purchased, but for a young child, a cardboard or wooden box will serve the purpose just as adequately. There is probably no finer container for a young, budding carpenter's tools than an empty cardboard beer case, the type with tops that fold in from both sides and lock in the center. These cartons are light enough for children to tote and are easily individualized with a bit of paint.

BUILDING AND GROWING

The treehouse-play apparatus on page 123 is part of the Residential Treatment Center play area, located four miles west of the University of South Florida. Residents of the Center, emotionally disturbed boys ranging in age from ten to seventeen years, helped in the design and construction. Imagination, organization, creativity, motor skills, leadership, a sense of accomplishment, recognition, personal satisfaction and self assurance are some of the traits developed in children while building a play structure such as the one at the Residential Treatment Center.

The Center's treehouse deck rises seven feet above the ground on four 4x4 pressure-treated posts. Each post, treated by the boys with a wood preservative coating, measures ten feet and is set in concrete. The floor joists and bracing are 2"x8" timber fastened together with ½"x4" hex bolts. These, in turn, connect to the 4"x4" uprights with ½"x6" hex bolts. Side and top rails are built from 2"x4" wood. The under-framework is also 2"x4" timber with 2"x4" planking spaced ⅜" apart to create the decking.

The boys designed and built into the structure a number of ways to ascend and descend from the deck including a metal pole, a hinged ladder and a ½" nylon rope net. Two slides, each located on different sides of the deck, allow for even quicker descents. One of the slides is eleven feet long and four feet wide. A covering of ⅛" high-density polyethylene adds to its life. On the other side of the platform, a 24 inch diameter, ten foot long fiberglass tube slide offers a speedy, self-contained route to the natural bed of leaf-covered soil below. This natural insulation cushions possible falls and sliding accidents.

A metal pole, ladder, rope net and two slides give youngsters a variety of ways to climb up and descend from this mighty platform. (Courtesy Michael Silverstein.)

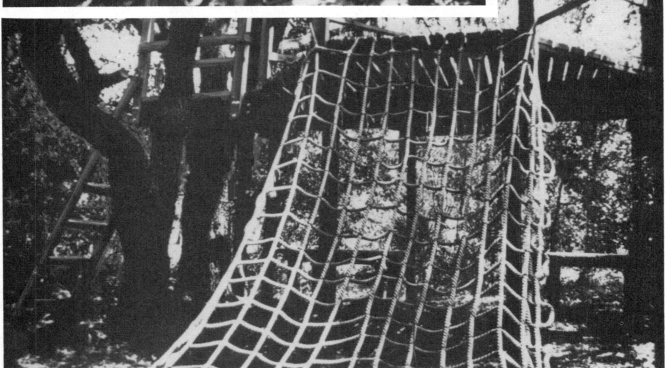

STICK DWELLINGS

As a small boy, I lived in a town about forty miles south of San Francisco. When my family moved to Los Altos, prune orchards dominated the countryside. Everywhere one looked there were prune trees. In the late summer months, the smell of the ripening fruit permeated the air for miles around. Needless to say, we consumed prune jam, prune juice, canned prunes, baked prunes and sliced and diced prunes until they were running out of our ears. But all that soon came to an end with tract homes. The orchards were cut down, the acreage divided into plots, and new homes constructed.

Playing in the skeletal, half-finished houses was great fun. Those building sites provided us with hours of running, climbing and hiding as well as many bruises. But there were also uprooted trees in those decimated orchards that kept us creatively busy. The things a kid can do with a pile of uprooted trees are truly amazing. Our forays into those topsy-turvy jungles consisted mainly of climbing and swinging among the enmeshed branches. Later, we discovered that cavernous forts and secret hideouts could be hacked out of the insides of these fallen trees. Secret chambers were interconnected by low passageways known only to the builders. Hollowing out our caverns was fairly easy, but the thorniest problem was getting rid of the useless branches and limbs. They invariably got entangled with healthy trees as we tried to drag them out into the open, away from our hide out. Scratched and branded by their sharp ends, we usually triumphed, often creating smaller, but equally impressive mounds of severed tree parts.

Suddenly one day, an idea struck four of us at the same time. Discarded branches could also be fashioned into forts and shacks. By chance we had stumbled onto the art of stick building.

One of the very first shelters we "instinctively" built consisted of four up-right branches, notched on one end and driven into the ground at the corners of an imaginary square. Four straight limbs were laid on top of these corner posts, resting snugly in the notched ends. These branches formed the frame for the roof and the walls. The level roof was little more than sticks laid lengthwise across the frame. We made the walls by resting additional sticks on the frame and at a slight angle so that they remained in place without any fastenings. Meticulously, we covered this framework with leafy remnants and in the end we had a super clubhouse that impressed our friends and served us well.

Over the months we experimented with other designs and developed several more unique structures. Then one of the boy's fathers showed us pictures of closely related shelters in the encyclopedia. Also pictured were designs for countless shelters made from raw, "wilderness" materials. Most of the designs, according to the text, had been perfected hundreds of years before by the American Indians. Our pride paled somewhat when we learned that our creations weren't originals. But we were soon back in the orchard/housing tract, testing out as many of the new designs as we could.

What follows are two of our favorite structures, the White Mountain Apache Hogan and the California Indian Tipi Hut, both of which can be duplicated by most kids with access to a few pruned limbs and branches (incidently, the first dwelling we stumbled across was a Pima Indian Lodge). Fortunately, you don't need uprooted orchards to build these playhouses. Collect together your own set of limbs and branches from home and neighborhood trimmings, park or highway departments or builders who are clearing sites.

WHITE MOUNTAIN APACHE HOGAN

Take two sturdy notched limbs and drive them into the ground four to six feet apart. Locate a stout-looking center beam and lay it into the notches of the two end supports. Rest as many smaller twigs as you can against the center beam, slanting them out towards the ground as in the walls of a tent. Apaches used a thatch of grass to cover this structure. Corn stalks work well, too.

CALIFORNIA INDIAN TIPI HUT

This was one of our favorites, mainly because we lived in California and could easily imagine ourselves as Indians guarding the sacred prune orchard from evil spirits. The Tipi also was simple to make. Interlock three forked sticks and drive their butts into the ground at the points of an equilateral triangle. Now lay a number of equally long limbs up against the forks of your original three so that their ends inscribe a circle in the ground. When the mood struck us and we had a bit more patience than usual, we'd weave smaller twigs through the larger branches, forming a tight latticework throughout the Tipi. Once we even coated the outside with mud, insuring our privacy and providing us with several hours of great fun (although I don't recall my parents being that enthusiastic on our mud-spattered return home that evening).

With a bit of imagination, you and your 9-13-year-olds can build untold numbers of these "primitive" shelters in a relatively short amount of time. For ideas, look in encyclopedias, history books, and those big picture books dealing with architecture. A particularly fun book with hundreds of pictures is *Shelter*, by Shelter Publications, P.O. Box 279, Bolinas, California 94924.

INDIAN BACK-REST

Outfitting these stick shelters was rarely a problem because we sat on the ground. In moments of extravagance, we'd throw an old, discarded rug or piece of carpet over the dusty ground and sit in style. If the ground is damp or your kids just don't feel like sitting on the ground, they can make one of the most distinctive of all Indian furnishings, a lazy-back.

Traditionally made from willow shoots strung together with cords of heavy sinew and propped up with four 5' lengths of pole made from pine saplings, these back rests are as comfortable as rocking chairs.

The kids can make their own without the willow rods and pine saplings by substituting canvas and ¾" wood dowels. Cut the canvas to a length of five feet, tapering from 21" at the top to 36" at the bottom. Hang the heavy cloth from a tripod of four foot lengths of doweling, the canvas resting against two of the tripod legs. One foot of the canvas stretches out in front of the backing. Your kids can sit on the ground cover, lean back and enjoy the Indian stick house they've just built from scratch.

STONE COOKING

If mealtime rolls around, you and the older kids might want to cook up a feast Indian style. Prairie Indians used to boil their foods in a special way, using hot stones and the paunch of freshly killed game. You can pick up the paunch from a local butcher shop. Clean it so that only the stomach lining remains. Either fasten the paunch bag-like on a quadripod made from four upright poles or lay it into the ground in a hole dug to size. Fill half-full with water and add chopped meat and vegetables.

In the meantime, heat fist-sized stones you've collected from the surrounding area. The stones should be thoroughly dry. Avoid picking up anything that resembles sandstone, flint or quartz. These stones, when hot, will either disintegrate or burst apart when placed in the paunch's water. You might want to test the stones before cooking to make sure they won't fly apart on you. Simply heat on a fire and place in a pot full of air-temperature water.

When the previously tested stones are good and hot, pick one from the fire using one or two forked branches and drop it into the paunch. Once the water has stopped hissing and bubbling, add another stone, and then another and so on. The toughest piece of meat will be thoroughly cooked within ½ hour.

STACK-SACKING

Stack-sacking is another building process where the kids should be allowed to do most of the designing, a lot of the building and most of the finishing work. Stack sacks are burlap bags of dry concrete piled into the shape your kids want. Sandbox walls, tunnels, cave playhouses, climbing hills and just about anything can be made with stack sacks. Of course, you're going to need quite a few burlap bags and pre-mixed concrete (a substitute for premixed concrete consists of sand, gravel, and dry cement in a ratio of 5:5:1). And you'll have to live with whatever you build since knocking down a stack-sack structure takes more effort than putting one up.

Burlap bags filled with concrete can be fashioned into any desired shape, from planters to tunnels and caves.

Decide on the shape of your space, then start stacking. Reinforce all sacks with metal rods driven through the bags into the ground. Tunnels can be formed by stacking the sacks over 55 gallon drums or forming arches with metal construction rods. Once you've got the desired shape, wet the sacks thoroughly. Frequent wetting will help prevent cracking while the structure dries. Keep the sacks damp for several days.

When you're sure the concrete is completely dry, plaster the surface of your creation. Because vertical walls and over-hangs are difficult to plaster, tack down chicken wire before the concrete is rock-hard. Now the kids are ready to apply the mortar. The wet plaster surface can be decorated with drawings and mosaics of broken tile, bottle caps, plastic scraps, rocks or whatever the children can embed in the plaster.

ADVENTURE PLAYGROUNDS

Adventure playgrounds are a kid's best friend. "But what's an adventure playground?", you ask. One of the most concise descriptions you'll find anywhere is given by the National Playing Fields Association in London: "An adventure playground is a place where children of all ages, under friendly supervision, are free to do many things they can no longer easily do in our crowded urban society: lighting fires and cooking; tree climbing, digging, camping; perhaps gardening and keeping animals; as well as playing team games, group games, painting, dressing up, modeling, reading . . . or doing nothing."

Adventure playgrounds can provide exciting opportunities for play in your own backyard.

C.T. Sorenson, a prominent landscape architect, built the first adventure playground in a suburb of Copenhagen in 1943 after he noticed

*In your backyard adventure play area, old tires, used building materials, and ropes can be built into play structures by the children themselves. (Designers are Nicholas Quennell Associates. Courtesy **A Playground for All Children**, New York Department of City Planning.)*

that children preferred to play in his conventional playgrounds while they were under construction more than after they were cleaned-up and finished. "Junkyard" and "Waste Material" are just some of the names attached to Sorenson's creations. And for good reason! Adventure play areas do, indeed, resemble shanty towns or junk yards.

Fastidious grown-ups may find adventure playgrounds noisy, bothersome and distracting eyesores. But there's more to adventure than meets the eyes and ears. Underneath all the boards, planks, and crates lies a release from the structured atmosphere that surrounds most traditional play areas. Structure, formal teaching and guidance are important components for positive growth and development. But, in every child there also is a strong need for informality; freedom of movement and expression; experimentation; and, imaginative and constructive play.

Freedom of choice allows all kinds of problems to arise that require children to apply their native ingenuity and skill. Children develop skills and techniques through these confrontations that help to positively shape their characters.

You can help nurture these same positive qualities in your children at home. Allow time in your offspring's day when they are free to make their own decisions about what they want to work on and how to go about it. Many of the playhouses and building techniques already described in this book can be the center for your own backyard adventure area. Stick houses, cardboard and tire carpentry, yurts, panel construction, block play all lend themselves to hours of creative play for kids three to sixteen.

TOOL STORAGE

An unending supply of wood, nails, paints, other building materials and tools enhance adventure play areas. Some of the most unlikely discards of civilization become prime ingredients for backyard adventures.

A safe place to store tools outside is in the impressive movable "tool shed" shown on page 128, designed by the folks at the Fountain Head School in Orinda, California. Actually, the "shed" is two boxes fashioned from exterior grade plywood and hinged together. There's enough room inside for all the tools the kids will ever need onsite in their adventure play area. The

Wheels allow kids to move this large tool chest from work area to work area. The chest locks up for safe storage.

two small chests at the bottom pull out and can be toted from one work area to another. When a project calls for more tools than can be lugged comfortably in the chests, the whole shed can be rolled into place on the two hard-rubber wheels up front.

The tools listed below are basic for most youngsters and will allow them to handle a wide variety of projects. Be sure to demonstrate the proper use of each one.

BASIC TOOLS FOR CHILDREN

Aluminum level	Surform shaver
Coping saw	C-clamps
Vise	Hammer (13 oz.)
Cross cut saw (20")	Pocket surform
Hand drill	Screwdrivers
Combination square	Bar clamp
¾" chisel	Tape ruler

BACKYARD STORAGE

All children will benefit the most from their adventure play yard when proper storage areas are provided. The tool chest on this page is an example of a well-designed unit. But it's certainly not large enough for all the tools and toys that can accumulate.

When building a larger storage unit, remember that the aim of storage is to segregate objects and make them as accessible as possible. Additional points to keep in mind are to: 1. build shallow; deep spaces encourage junking and make it difficult to see what's stored (you can construct walk-in storage units, but remember to keep the shelves shallow and the passageways uncluttered); 2. avoid using an existing playhouse or climbing structure for storage because the kids have to pull everything out before playing on or in it.

The unit below was designed by the Canadian Children's Environments Advisory Service. Sit down with your kids and use this design as a springboard for planning a storage space that satisfies the needs of your backyard play environment. A well-designed storage unit can make the difference between a little-used play area and one that jumps with creative activity.

Storage Area. (Courtesy Canadian Children's Environments Advisory Service.) See page 130 for details.

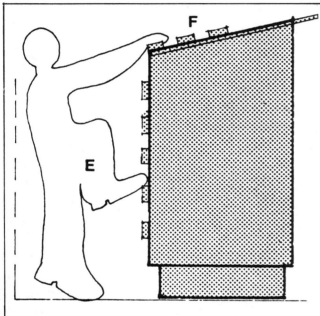

A. Overall dimensions: 2'0''x8'0''x3'0'' (600x2400x900 mm), sloping up to 3'6'' (1050 mm) high at front with slight overhang.

B. Doors to be lockable.

C. Sturdy support for shelves for miscellaneous play equipment.

D. Storage for 4'0'' (1200 mm) ladders and boards of various sizes. Pieces of tarpaulin can be used to throw over boards at night and become play material during the day.

E. End elevation shows 2'0'' (600 mm) minimum space behind to allow children access to climb on roof.

F. 2''x3'' (38x65 mm) hardwood blocks fixed to unit to assist in climbing.

SAFETY

No backyard adventure play area will work without parental intervention and supervision. As a parent and primary caretaker, you should check that every construction project is safe, even long after it is completed. Look for frayed ropes, pull out dangerous nails, dispose of rusty metal and broken glass. Ask the kids to help you. If you spot a loose wall, for example, ask the children how they might make it stronger.

Your duties as a parent go beyond checking for safety, though. There'll be many times when you're called upon to listen, guide, help and protect. An illustrative and colorful story is told by an English adventure playground leader.

"A vivid experience I remember on our playground involved Tommy, a little boy, four or five-years-old, who asked to be put on the twenty-foot rope swing which swung out over a fifteen-foot drop in the hillside. I picked him up and sat him in the knot. That's all I did. Then he said, 'Push me'. I had not seen him on the swing before, so I cautiously pushed him just out of hand's reach. He had been quite calmly sitting on the knot, but now he was screwed into a tight little ball, his face set rigid in terror. I was terrified as well, because I didn't really want to frighten the little guy. He obviously was not enjoying himself, so I stilled him. Relaxing slightly, he said again, 'Push me'. I wondered what was going on because I could not match his words with his terror. This time as the swing slowed, the terror abated and he looked a little happier, his lips had turned up in a slight smile. The third time as he slowed down, he relaxed and even eased back on the rope before he again said, 'Push me'. He was putting himself into a situation which he did not fully understand, did not enjoy, but which he wanted to learn about and had seen others enjoy. Within a week no one could push him high enough, the sky was his limit. He trusted the rope because I had put him on it, not because he knew I checked it every day for wear. Within the safety limits provided by me he still had to discover and conquer his own fear."

HANDICAPPED CHILDREN AND ADVENTURE PLAY

Handicapped children benefit from backyard adventure play, too. Adventure playgrounds for handicapped children in England are very popular and successful. Kids with physical, mental and emotional disabilities have gained self-confidence and benefited from challenges traditionally denied them.

Many of these kids will need constant reassurance before they can venture alone with a minimum of adult help. But the rewards are great, many youngsters learn through physical experience when "book learning" is still extremely difficult.

As with all other play structures intended for use by handicapped children, certain material and design considerations must be met. All pieces of equipment must be built to withstand constant battering by children confined to wheelchairs, crutches, etc. Doorways, especially, are very vulnerable to wear and tear. Keep your kids in mind when it comes to door widths, access to partially raised structures and the height of workbenches, sand and water tables. The simplest rule to remember is to "think of your children" when building.

Manufacturers' List

Ideas for successful playhouses often come from watching children at play. Do the kids climb trees a lot? Perhaps a backyard jungle gym or a treehouse will best suit their needs. You also can get additional ideas for play spaces from the catalogs of toy and playground equipment manufacturers. Some of the manufacturers' catalogs listed below can be picked up at local toy stores or school supply outlets. If none are available in your area, write directly to the manufacturer and request information on obtaining the catalog (be sure to enclose a self-addressed, stamped envelope for a prompt reply).

American Playground Device Co.
P.O. Drawer 2599
Anderson, Indiana 46011
Playground equipment

American Toy & Furniture Co., Inc.
5933-T N. Lincoln Avenue
Chicago, Illinois 60659
Wood

Baker Mfg. Co.
Columbia, Pennsylvania 17512
Tool, kitchen, etc.

Brown Group, Inc.
8400 Maryland Avenue
St. Louis, Missouri 63105
Furniture

Cadaco, Inc.
310 W. Polk
Chicago, Illinois 60607
Educational

Carnival Toys, Inc.
450 Hancock Avenue
Bridgeport, Connecticut 06605
Educational

Childcraft Education Corp.
20 Kilmer Road
Edison, New Jersey 08817
Educational

Child Life Play Specialities, Inc.
55 Whitney Street
Holliston, Massachusetts 01746
Outdoor play equipment

Coleco Industries, Inc.
945 Asylum Avenue
Hartford, Connecticut 06105
Educational

Connor Forest Industries
P.O. Box 847
Wausau, Wisconsin 54401
Table sets, doll furniture

Constructive Playthings
1040 East 85th Street
Kansas City, Missouri 64131
Outdoor equipment, educational, Special education

Creative Playthings
A Division of CBS, Inc.
Edinburg Road
Cranbury, New Jersey 08512
Educational

Creative Technology Aids
30 Warren Street
Brighton, Massachusetts 02135
Special Education (electromagnetic toys)

Dakin, R. & Co.
499-T Pt. San Bruno Blvd.
South San Francisco, California 94080
General

De Kalb Toys, Inc.
De Kalb, Illinois 60115
Wood

Developmental Learning Materials
7440 Natchez Avenue
Niles, Illinois 60648
Special Education

Earl & Arlington Inc.
582 Market
San Francisco, California 94104
Crib Toys

Edmund Scientific Co.
7897 Edscrop Bldg.
Barrington, New Jersey 08007
Scientific

Educational Playsystems Div.
200 5th Avenue
New York, New York 10010
Educational

Educational Toy Co.
2305-T Louisiana Avenue N.
Minneapolis, Minnesota 55427
Educational

Eldon Industries, Inc.
2701-T El Segundo Blvd.
Hawthorne, California 90250
General

Ergonomix
P.O. Box 3216
San Leandro, California 94578
Special Education

Ertl Company, The
805 13th Avenue, S.E.
Dyersville, Iowa 52040
Farm Toys

Exceptional Child Development Center, Inc.
725 Liberty Avenue
Pittsburg, Pennsylvania 15222
Special Education

Exceptional Play
P.O. Box 1015
Lawrence, Kansas 66044
Special Education

Fisher-Price Toys
606 Girard Avenue
East Aurora, New York 14052
Preschool wood & plastic action, push & pull, building blocks

Gabriel Industries, Inc.
200 Fifth Avenue
New York, New York 10010
Pre-school educational

Game-Time, Inc.
900 Anderson Road
Litchfield, Michigan 49252
Wood playground equipment

General Mills, Inc.
P.O. Box 1113
Minneapolis, Minnesota 55440
Crafts & Games

Gilbert Industries, Inc.
Long Meadow Road
P.O. Box 980
Hagerstown, Maryland 21740
Educational

Grey Iron Casting Co.
P.O. Box 40
Wrightsville, Pennsylvania 17368
Tool sets, stoves, utensils, tool chests

Happy Hour Playground Equipment Co.
805 Moore
Baraboo, Wisconsin 53913
Slides, teeters, gyms, swings

Holbrook-Patterson, Inc.
Monroe at Maxie-Club
Coldwater, Michigan 49036
Educational

Howell Playground Equipment Co.
1718 E. Fairchild Street
Danville, Illinois 61832
Swings, slides, ladders, etc.

Humenick's Wood Products Mfg. Co.
R.D. 1, Box 14-T
Weatherly, Pennsylvania 18255
Wood

Ideal School Supply Co.
11000 S. Lavergne Avenue
Oak Lawn, Illinois 60453
Educational

Island Industries
Box 96
Cos Cob, Connecticut 06807
Wooden

Judy Co.
310 N. 2nd Street
Minneapolis, Minnesota 55401
Instructional matirials for schools & homes

Kenmore Industries, Inc.
Woodbine Road
P.O. Box 155
Belmont, Massachusetts 02178
Wood

Knickerbocker Toy Co., Inc.
207 Pond Avenue
Middlesex, New Jersey 08846
Pre-school

Kransco Mfg., Inc.
464 Victory Avenue
South San Francisco, California 94080
General

Kusan, Inc.
3206 Belmont Blvd.
Nashville, Tennessee 37212
Blocks, pull toys

Marks, S. R. Co., Inc.
2600 Day Street
Montgomery, Alabama 36108
Plywood

Milton Bradley Co.
P.O. Box 3400
Springfield, Massachusetts 01101
General

Miracle Recreation Equipment Co.
P.O. Box 275 TR
Grinnell, Iowa 50112
Swings, climbers, slides, etc.

National School Slate Co.
7th & Church
Slatington, Pennsylvania 18080
Slate blackboards, chests, sandboxes, etc.

Outdoor Products Co.
1759 Smith Avenue
P.O. Box 24527
San Jose, California 95112
Playground equipment

Park Timber Co.
1914 Colvin Blvd.
Tonawanda, New York 14150
Play structures of wood and timber

Parker Brothers
50-T Dunham Road
Beverly, Massachusetts 01915
General

Patterson-Williams Mfg. Co.
651 Aldo Avenue
P.O. Box 4040
Santa Clara, California 95050
Outdoor athletic equipment

Plakie, Inc.
4105 Simon Road
Youngstown, Ohio 44512
Crib, nursery and bath toys

Playskool, Inc.
4501 W. Augusta Blvd.
Chicago, Illinois 60651
Wood and Plastic cars, blocks

Pre-School Press, Inc.
159 West 53rd Street
New York, New York 10019
Pre-school

Quality Industries, Inc.
P.O. Box 120T
Hillsdale, Michigan 49242
Commercial Playground Equipment

Recreation Equipment Corp.
8th and John Streets
Anderson, Indiana 46011
Swings, see saws, slides, climbing gyms

Rich Industries, Inc.
Tupelo, Mississippi 38801
Dollhouses, chests

Rose Art Industries
100 8th Street
Passaic, New Jersey 07055
Craft kits

Rotadyne, Inc.
8703 Freeway Drive
Cleveland, Ohio 44130
Storage chests, riding toys

Sanitoy, Inc.
150 Roosevelt Place
Palisades Park, New Jersey 07650
Infant toys

Skil Craft Corp.
P.O. Box 705
Racine, Wisconsin 53401
Educational

Skill Development Equipment Co.
Box 6300, 1340 North Jefferson
Anaheim, California 92807
Special Education

Special Education Materials, Inc.
484 South Broadway
Yonkers, New York 10705
Special Education

Toidey Co., Inc.
4320 Ardmoor
Fort Wayne, Indiana 46804
Table & chair sets, Doll Cribs & Cradles

Trojan Playground Equipment Mfg. Co.
11-T 2nd Avenue, N.E.
St. Cloud, Minnesota 56301
Indoor & outdoor slides, swings, bars, see saws, ladders, etc.

Whitney Bros. Co.
6 Water
Marlborough, New Hampshire 03455
Wooden pre-school Toys

Wilson Rollin Co.
P.O. Box 7433
Memphis, Tennessee 38107
Wood

Wolverine Toy Co.
Booneville, Arkansas 72927
Housekeeping, Action and Mechanical

Vaughan and Associates, Inc.
2852 Walnut Hill Lane
Dallas, Texas 75229
Playground equipment

Index